WHERE
WE
LAND

A Pilot's Reflections at Altitude

By Donald Osborn
with Anna Henkens Schmidt

"Most blurbs are dishonest, so I rarely concede to them *except* when I genuinely like a book, which is the case with *Where We Land*, a thoroughly detailed, well-crafted, humorous, sagacious, and refreshingly frank account of the many adventures, anecdotes, and arguments of an aviator, who has seen the wide world many times over and flown just about everything with wings except a pterodactyl."

-Poe Ballantine
Author of *Love and Terror on the Howling Plains of Nowhere*

Disclaimer: This memoir is a collection of hazy memories, half-baked anecdotes, and questionable life choices. If you find any inaccuracies, blame it on the following: aging brain cells, selective amnesia,
and too much time in the sky.

Permissions: You are allowed to chuckle heartily at my misadventures, share embarrassing excerpts with your book club, and to use this memoir as a very poor flotation device. You are not allowed to fact-check (seriously, don't ruin the fun), hold me accountable for any emotional trauma caused by faulty recollections, or attempt to replicate my life choices.

First paperback edition April 2024

ISBN-13: 979-8-9902833-0-5 (paperback)

Instagram: @where_we_land_book

This book is dedicated in memory

of our beloved mother, Loretta Henkens,

whose love fueled our flights to remarkable heights.

Table of Contents

Emergency Escape

I always had to look down.

The quietness of the cockpit purred with the almost indiscernible hum of the *Falcon 50's* three engines. Its metal wingspan stretched over the open plains, sliced through the wisps of clouds that glowed as the sun filtered through the delicate water droplets. I rested my hands needlessly on the control yoke, the jet's autopilot perfectly capable of navigating through the pale blue skies. My body also went into autopilot. The passengers might have thought that I, a seasoned pilot commanding a sophisticated machine, would be accustomed to a view like this.

But I had to look down.

Each time I flew over Western Nebraska, over the wheat fields of the rugged cattle country, over the tiny towns that could be missed in an insignificant blink, I never dared to shut my eyes. Nebraska's unofficial motto is *The Good Life*, but I still wondered about the people who settled here. Did they just get tired on their trek to California? Did they glimpse the incomprehensible mountains on the far west horizon and say to themselves, "Well, dang. I guess this is far enough?"

For some, it was *The Good Enough Life*. For me, Nebraska is a bit more complicated.

The compulsion to look down intensified.

It was as though by memorizing the placement of the town's water tower and perpendicular streets that I could somehow bring back the boy who wanted nothing more than to be where I am now. I looked down to the field where that boy discovered his first airplane. I looked down to the small airport where he walked in as a nobody and earned his first license.

I'd love to talk to him. Tell him that someday he'd fly the big jets of his dreams. He'd one day fly A-list movie stars and Presidents of the United States. One day, he'd finally be able to see all the corners of the world that only existed in his imagination.

But would I also have to warn him of the turbulence on the horizon?

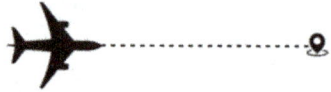

As a 14-year-old boy growing up in western Nebraska, nothing was more exciting than the idea of leaving western Nebraska. The idea was one that required an escape route. Some kids hoped to escape through the military or through advanced degrees at far away colleges; but the truth was, for a kid like me, there weren't a lot of options.

So I escaped through a machine shed at the edge of town.

The shed was owned by Ol' Frank, and though he kept it locked, the siding wasn't in tip-top shape. The first time I snuck into the shed, I was able to squeeze my adolescent body through a loose part of that siding. To most people, the inside of a machine shed might not seem like an escape. After all, I hadn't even left town.

But, I am not most people.

What I saw inside the shed was not only my escape route; it was my hopes, my dreams, and my plan to take me away from western Nebraska to the farthest reaches of the globe. Inside the shed, the smell of fuel, dirt, and droppings hit me—a smell that can still transport me today. The yellow *Piper J-3 Cub*, a tandem-seat airplane manufactured between 1938 and 1947, sat gleaming through the darkness of the shed. Black soot stuck to the end of the exhaust pipe of the small four-cylinder engine, which was bolted directly to a wooden prop. This model had originally been built as a trainer and as a general aviation aircraft. During World War II, the *Cub* was mass produced as the *L-4 Grasshopper*.

It was the most exciting thing I'd ever seen.

My head always turned skyward whenever I heard the familiar rumble, and I had tracked that yellow bird to Frank's field on the edge of town, and watched as he parked it in this very machine shed.

Sneaking into the shed became such a regular occurrence for me, I decided to make my door a little more permanent. Though I should mention that the siding that I'd been pulling back to squeeze through had finally snapped in half. With some old leather straps, some screws, and the broken piece of siding, I cobbled together a door that I was sure couldn't be seen from the outside.

I spent hours just sitting in that airplane, imagining what all the controls could do. Four gauges, a control stick, a throttle, and a seat were the escape route to my future. In my mind, I was already flying. With my eyes closed, and my hand clutched over the control stick, I saw myself in the sky, flying over friends' houses, tipping my wing at my mom who'd be outside hanging laundry in the ethereal breeze. She would look up and wave, smile with pride, and notice that I'd made something of myself. As the afternoon sun turned slantwise and illuminated the dancing dust motes in the shed, I lost track of my actual surroundings and instead traveled on long expeditions, finally learning what lay beyond the distant wheatfields and badlands. I was so spellbound in my reveries that I didn't hear the truck door shut right outside the shed, or the telltale sound of workboots crunching against gravel. I certainly didn't notice the door creak open.

"What the hell?"

My eyes popped open. There stood Frank, silhouetted in the doorframe.

Suddenly I needed a more immediate escape route.

I scrambled out of the airplane, hitting my shin on the way out. Ignoring the sharp pain, I threw myself towards the broken boards in the back and jammed my bony limbs through the emergency exit, picking up a few new splinters as the sound of heavy boots stalked behind me. Just as the last lace of my untied tennis shoes slipped through the crack, something heavy thudded against the side of the building. With a solid punt to the kickstand, I lunged onto my bicycle and pedaled my Buzz Bike down the trail away from the shed as hard as I could.

But I was no match for Frank's red 1969 F150 pickup. While his truck barreled behind me like an escaped demon, the wheels on my bike swerved out from under me. The next thing I knew, I was face-up in the field, looking skywards; but instead of a yellow airplane, all I could see was Frank's looming face and his white hair sticking out from under his baseball cap.

He stood so close that the smell of his chewing tobacco burned the inside of my nostrils. "So, you're the little son of a bitch that's been in my hangar."

2

$12 Ascent

I was five years-old the first time I boarded an airplane.

We were leaving Carson City, Nevada. My mom—arms filled with my infant brother, Stephen, and her watchful eyes on my toddler sisters, Theresa and Jeannette—accepted help from a stranger getting all of us aboard the *Douglas DC-3*. Our worldly possessions were packed inside bulging suitcases. Excitement hammered through my body, and it was impossible to sit still. I squirmed in my seat, my legs bouncing of their own accord.

It was my first escape by air.

We were escaping away from a broken marriage, away from Nevada, and heading to Nebraska. We flew at night, up close and personal with the stars. I'd always wondered what exactly was on those stars and felt slight disappointment that the stars looked the same from the sky as they did on the ground.

I forgot we were escaping anything as I looked through those dark, rectangular windows, the thrill pulsing through me, no doubt asking my mom a thousand questions she couldn't answer. But nothing mattered except the magic of 30,000 pounds flying 20,000 feet off the ground at 200 miles per hour. I knew then that I needed to be the one up front.

My parents, Don and Loretta Osborn, married straight out of high school. The football hero and the well-liked cheerleader of Hemingford, Nebraska, were a likely match from outside appearances. Both had dashing looks, thick dark hair, slim builds. My dad planned to teach and coach football. My mom wanted nothing more than to keep house and raise children.

The couple wasted no time in beginning their family. A devout Catholic, my mom believed it was her God-given duty to raise as many children in the faith as her womb would carry. She and Dad left Nebraska and drove across the country to Carson City, Nevada. From appearances, the young wife, still thin and beautiful after four children, and the handsome husband, who coached the local high school football team, were living the ideal existence. Though they didn't have a lot of money, they worked hard; the football team won more games than they lost, and they seemed happy.

But on Sunday mornings, the nuns began to notice my mom attending mass alone with her four small children. They noticed as her smile tightened and dark circles formed under her eyes. It became apparent that my dad was Catholic in name only and didn't subscribe to all the church's tenants, mainly the ones against adultery, gambling, and drunkenness.

Stubborn in her faith, Mom stayed with him, doing her best to raise four kids in a hellish household. It wasn't until the nuns convinced my mom divorce was her best option that she finally took her leave.

My memories of the inner workings of my family life at that time are mostly fuzzy recollections. I do clearly remember watching airplanes fly overhead.

Ol' Frank stood over me, his looming presence eclipsing the sun.

I was convinced he was going to kill me. My last moments on this earth, and I'd die on my back in a field on the edge of town, any hope of escape thwarted.

"Can you operate a Farmall tractor, boy?"

His question caught me so off-guard all I could do was squeak.

"Can you operate a Farmall tractor with a mower?" Frank repeated.

My brain was slowly catching up, but the answer was obvious. In the early '70s in western Nebraska, it was unimaginable that a 14-year-old boy could not drive a tractor. "Yes, sir," I said.

"In that case," Frank said. "You'd better get to work."

Twenty minutes later I was out on the tractor, mowing the makeshift runway. Not a bad way to break into the world of aviation.

Frank and I agreed that seven days of hard labor on his farm would about cover the damage I had done to the side of his machine shed. Lucky for me, I was raised by a mother whose work ethic was second to none, work being the primary goal in her life. Work you did yesterday or the work you planned to do tomorrow meant nothing to her. The only work that mattered was the amount of work that was being done at the moment.

As hard as Ol' Frank tried to work me, it was nothing compared to what my mom expected of me on a daily basis.

The seven days went by quickly, and the first day I walked through the door of the shed instead of crawling inside on my belly would prove to be a pinnacle turning point for me. I would no longer need that secret trap door on the side of the building. My aviation career was about to take off.

Frank could have reported me to the cops, threatened me with physical harm, or banned me from his property. Worse, he could have told my mom. Instead, he took a different approach. For $12 an hour, he'd teach me to fly. I am happy that my youthful mind did not calculate the logic of how long and hard it would be to come up with $12 on a regular basis. I had a job in town working at Harry's Conoco for $0.75 an hour washing windshields, pumping gas, checking oil, scrubbing floors, and whatever else they could get the lowest employees to do. But the combination of big hopes and bigger dreams proved greater than logic and math. Looking back at my first logbook, you can see a flight lesson every seven to ten days.

People always want to know if at any point I experienced fear when it came to flying. I think back to those days, and the answer is yes. Showing up for a flight lesson without the $12 was the most fear-inducing part of flying that I've experienced. After the first couple of lessons, Frank always wanted the money in advance to make sure I had it.

The first time Frank took me up in the J3, the wheat fields and cow pastures miniaturized below me, and I felt like I'd grown into something of a giant. I felt such exhilaration being in the air, doing something that not too many people had done, especially not in my pint-sized town that grew smaller with each foot climbed. Before I'd even had time to fully take in my surroundings, Frank turned the controls over to me. In my mind, I'd imagined grasping at the controls, manhandling the machine as though I'd stolen it. But it turns out that an airplane is flown with just a couple of fingers, a technique of applying slight pressure to make small adjustments. This was just a gentle handing over, Frank turning his life and machine over to me, without the amount of concern and trepidation he probably should've displayed.

I breathed in the distinct scent of the old airplane—stale air and must, combined with burned fuel. A small airplane is noisy, and the consuming rumble of the engine encased me in a world far away from everything I'd known. When we landed, I looked yearningly up to the sky and knew I'd do whatever I needed to get back up there.

3

Skybound Delinquent

Ol' Frank soloed me after eight hours.

He told me to take the *Cub* around the patch two or three times, come back, clean the bugs off the airplane, sweep out the hangar, and put the airplane away.

I'm not sure he even stood around to watch. No doubt there was work to be done, and he didn't have time to see that I made it back in one piece.

Today, the typical student doesn't fly solo until they're at least 16 years old and have completed between 15 and 20 hours of airtime with an instructor. Most instructors will stand and watch the first few takeoffs and landings. Some airports even have a little building near the runway that resembles a chapel. They call this the instructor's prayer house. If Frank was praying for me that day, he didn't let me know.

If I'd known then what I know today, I never would have agreed to take out an airplane after only eight hours of instruction at the tender age of 14. Though one of the advantages of being a 14-year-old boy is that you believe yourself to be indestructible. You believe you can fly an airplane after only $96 worth of lessons. You believe you probably could have flown the airplane without any instructions in the first place. If I'd known then what I know today, I wouldn't have been in that plane making decisions at a higher level than ever before, making decisions that my life depended on, decisions that held actual weight.

But up there, I felt weightless. And I made all those decisions with a big smile on my face.

The second time I soloed an airplane, I snuck a friend on board. You'd think my friends would all have been smart enough to outright turn me down, but for whatever reason, Mike Carson said he'd go along with me. When I was sure Frank was otherwise occupied, I motioned for Mike, and he tiptoed over and slipped inside. My first solo flight had been such a thrill, I just had to share the adventure.

Once I got the plane in the air, I brought it back down into some low-level buzz work, meaning I flew too close to the ground, skimming over people's houses and terrestrial obstructions. Not only was this unsafe, it was also terrifically illegal. The regulations for altitude vary from air space to air space, but what I did that day was against regulations in every stratosphere. Advantages of low-level flying include splendid views and an adrenaline rush. Disadvantages of low-level flying include not being able to see as far ahead, increasing the risk of collision with terrain or obstacles—such as electrical wires, the expanded probability of both thermal and mechanical turbulence, reduced reaction time, decreased distance to execute an emergency landing, and an escalated chance of hitting birds.

No doubt, it was probably the most dangerous thing I've ever done in an airplane. But I wasn't doing it to be rebellious, or even to prove myself to anyone. I did it because it was fun. And mostly I did it because I didn't know any better. Many times over the years, I explained to Mike how close to death he came that day. But as dumb as I was in that moment, I'm still glad we got to experience that adventure in the sky together.

Frank continued schooling me, but his method of teaching was laid-back, to say the least.

Today there are four main stages in flight training. The first stage is the pre-solo stage, which consists of individual flight lessons in the basic operations of the airplane. The completion of this stage would be the student's first solo flight. The second stage is the dual cross-country stage, when the student makes a combination of flights with the instructor to destinations more than 50 nautical miles from the home airport. The student learns navigation skills, various landings such as short and soft field landings, crosswind, and emergency landings, as well as night flight and other procedures essential for cross-country trips. Once these have been perfected with the instructor, the student would then move onto the third stage, which is the solo cross-country stage–trips that you plan and execute yourself, with oversight and review from your instructor. The final stage is the preparation for the Federal Aviation Administration (FAA) Flight Test.

Frank's dual cross-country training consisted of telling me we needed to fly to Douglas, Wyoming, to pick up a part for a tractor. He must have felt confident with my one and only flight with him in the co-pilot seat because several days later he handed me a roadmap and said I should go to Sturgis, South Dakota, and then to Gordon, Nebraska, then once I made it back to Chadron, he'd count that as my first solo cross-country. Confident and eager to please, I headed for Sturgis and successfully landed at the airport in Spearfish, South Dakota, 20 miles from my intended destination. My eyes bugged out of my head when my logbook was signed and I saw that I had not, in fact, landed in Sturgis. Undeterred, I headed to Gordon with little-to-no navigation skills. I found Rushville, Nebraska, which was 15 miles off my mark. Feeling a bit anxious, I circled the plane around the town's water tower. I decided that my best bet would be to just follow the highway back to Chadron, where I'd at least be able to land in a familiar location. I kept my eyes on the dotted yellow line of the highway below me and didn't pay much attention to the fuel gauge.

Once I arrived back in Chadron, Frank said, "Good, you figured it out, but you should have refueled in Gordon." I had landed with only 20 minutes of fuel on board, but I didn't have the heart to tell him that I'd never made it to Gordon.

Remembering that trip today causes me far more anxiety than it ever did at the time, mostly because I didn't know enough to be scared. A pilot with any know-how will read that account and feel a ball of stress start to roll around in the bottom of his gut. It takes experience to think about what might have happened. It's like a kid picking up a chainsaw for the first time. He'd have no concept of RPMs, kickback, or the power involved in a two-cycle engine, but he could definitely see that tree falling down when he was cutting into it. An adult seeing that kid with a chainsaw would have a pretty good visual of all the things that could go wrong.

Over the years I've driven through those small Highway 20 towns east of Chadron, and it always brings a smile to my face, knowing that I'd accomplished my first solo-cross country with such a lack of aviation knowledge.

Mom's purse barely opened wide enough to keep us all clothed and fed, and she'd likely have been pissed as hell if she'd known I was spending good money for flight lessons. Already she was doing everything she could to keep our family going. Usually she'd already polished off her first pot of coffee, finished a load of laundry, baked up a batch of homemade bread, cleaned the house, and started dinner before we'd even gotten out of bed. She'd taken in foster kids from the Pine Ridge Reservation, mostly out of the goodness of her heart, but also to collect the check that went along with it. She hired herself out as a house cleaner to the town's wealthier residents, and as a nursemaid to more than one homebound elderly patient. She even cleaned the American Legion, the Elk's Club, and the tractor company east of town, Henkens Implement, where years later she'd marry the owner, Earl Henkens. She took in ironing, sold her fresh-baked bread, made and sold stuffed animals, altered clothing, and canned at least 400 quarts of food every year from her garden. When gas was only $0.36 a gallon, she'd drive us kids around so we could collect bottles. She made a deal with a local farmer's wife to butcher all her chickens in exchange for free meat.

No job was below her.

Sometimes she'd pretend she wasn't hungry and skip dinner, rather than admit there wasn't enough food to go around. In the summers, she would drive us out to Chadron State Park so we could go swimming, and she'd sit outside of the chain-linked fence in the hot sun, watching us so she wouldn't have to pay the $0.25 entry fee. When she had the energy, she'd come to our games and school plays. She'd show up at the cafeteria and volunteer to serve the hot lunch fundraisers. She'd always make sure that we had our own hot lunches waiting for us at home each day. When my sisters wanted new clothes, but couldn't afford the latest fashions, my mom spent hours over her sewing machine, attempting to replicate what was in the JCPenney catalog.

Chadron was not and is not a big town, and there are few secrets among its residents, so it's a mystery if she truly didn't know about my flying, or if she purposely chose ignorance. At any rate, I didn't tell her I was learning to fly until years later when I had my commercial pilot's license and 250 hours in my logbook.

As the oldest of four children, I had a bit more leeway than my siblings. Mom only had so much energy, so I think she chose to trust me, attempting to save her parenting prowess to stretch over the younger flock. In truth, I wanted her to take notice of me, to take more of an interest in what interested me. I wanted her to pause from scrubbing the kitchen floor on her hands and knees and see me. I didn't understand at the time, but for Mom, work was her escape. She was ashamed of her status as a divorced woman, which was difficult for any woman at that time, but especially difficult for a devout Catholic. She escaped into work, seeking absolution through exhaustion, perhaps worried that she would never find it from God.

If I'd been an ideal first-born son, I might've turned over my earnings to help lighten my mom's load. Or perhaps I would have stayed at home more to help around the house. Maybe I would have done more to take care of my siblings, rather than allowing my responsibilities to fall on their shoulders. But I was young, and I was selfish, and I had my own escape plan.

Rather than fall in line, I used my mom's deficits to my advantage, which did not earn me a reputation as a model citizen in Chadron. When friends and acquaintances found out I was learning to fly, I could almost see a cartoon bubble float out of the top of their heads, "God help us all."

Evidently Frank was immune to my rumored

reputation because he began offering me two hours of free flying if I'd deliver medical supplies to a farmer who lived far out in the country. I eagerly took these opportunities, always yearning for more hours in the sky. I probably flew 20 hours in Frank's plane, but I spent hundreds of hours in his hangar, and will always remember that old machine shed as the place where aviation seemed to me the greatest adventure that a young juvenile delinquent could experience.

4

Flight of the Finagler

After a lot of fun hours, but not very much instruction, Frank decided I should go to the big airport and take serious lessons.

To give some perspective, that 'big' airport was five miles west of town. Encompassing 716 acres and featuring two concrete runways, Chadron Municipal Airport was surrounded by cattle pastures and farmsteads, and was staffed by a handful of people in 1973. Compare this to Denver International Airport, located about five hours west of Chadron. Boasting the largest square footage of any airport in the country and second largest in the world, DIA sits on approximately 34,560 acres, and employs more than 35,000 employees. This is especially jaw-dropping when considering that the entire town of Chadron covers only 2,496 acres and has 5,229 residents according to the 2021 census.

But that little Chadron airport seemed downright huge to me.

I borrowed a red Cushman scooter and headed west. Barely 16 years old, and with only about 20 hours of flying experience to my name, I rode those five miles assuming I'd be hired as a pilot on the spot.

After parking the scooter outside, I walked into the modest fix-based operator (FBO). Three pairs of eyes fastened on me as I entered. I'd put on my best bib overalls for the occasion but hadn't bothered with a shirt underneath. My hair was shoulder-length and no doubt disheveled from my highway scooter ride.

One of the men, who I later learned was the FBO owner, Jim Strang, offered a very polite, "May I help you?"

I looked around and boldly stated that I was there to get a pilot job.

Jim pulled me aside, "So, you're a pilot?"

"Yeah," I said, dropping my eyes down to my shoes.

"Well, what can you fly?"

I looked up and saw a *Taylor Craft* that was sitting on the ramp, thinking it was just the white version of Frank's yellow *J-3 Cub*. I pointed to the plane.

I figured that in no time at all that I'd be offered a job, so it wasn't a surprise when Jim said, "Let's go fly this thing." Upon entering the plane, I got my first indication that this wasn't a *Cub*. Instead of the two seats being one in front of the other, this plane featured side-by-side seating. Additionally, the standard control stick I'd become accustomed to was replaced by a control wheel, similar to a car's steering wheel, for aileron (longitudinal axis) and elevator (lateral axis) control. I'd never landed a plane on pavement, nor had I ever seen a radio inside an airplane. There were likely procedures to fly this thing, but I didn't have the first idea what they were.

I don't remember a lot of specifics about that flight, but we went up, we came back down, and we lived to tell the tale. Back on the ground, I followed him into his office, bracing myself for a series of questions.

"Do you own a shirt?"

"Yes, sir."

"Will you cut your hair?"

I nodded.

"I'll be honest with you. You flew the airplane about

as well as anybody at your age, but you know the least about aviation of anyone I've ever met."

He offered me a job on the spot, just as I'd hoped.

It was not the pilot job I'd been hoping for. Instead, he handed me a broom and gave me the title of 'hangar sweeper' and whatever other odd jobs he found for me to do.

Though I was getting paid to do the grunt work around the airport, it wouldn't be enough to cover all my expenses. The more I learned about aviation, the lighter my pockets felt. To get to the point where I could make a living in this career, I'd need to obtain numerous licenses, certifications, and log enough hours. My best bet to earn money while still learning to fly was to become a Certified Flight Instructor. But even this would require time, lessons, and money. Just for starters I'd need flight lessons to earn my private, instrument, and commercial pilot's licenses. This would include ground school and flight instruction, which entails a pre-brief and debrief with the instructor, and though this mostly just involves standing around by the airplane and talking through the flight, that extra time would come directly out of my wallet.

I'd have to be resourceful. To get to where I wanted to go, I'd have to do some finagling. I'd already finagled a door on the side of a machine shed to get closer to my aviation goals. Finagling wasn't a problem.

I shoveled snow, mowed lawns, worked on farms, delivered farm equipment ... any odd job I could find. I was hired as an on-air personality at our local AM 610 radio station. My friend, Kenny Groves, an equally resourceful high schooler, started his own tree trimming business, which remains successful today. Kenny would gladly work me until I couldn't see straight whenever I had extra hours in my day.

Jim's flight school consisted of a charter pilot who doubled as a flight instructor. For whatever reason, these pilots didn't stay around long. Many quit after months or even weeks. Notably, a couple of them quit after only a few days. Because of this rotating cast of characters, I can't remember most of their names; but they each had different styles, ways of doing things, or particularities that took getting used to. While I got along fine with all of them, it meant more work for me, as each instructor felt the need to retest certain skills to make sure I really knew what I was doing. More time equals more money. In the long run, this was likely a benefit and helped me to become a better pilot, but at the time it frustrated my purposes.

The written exam for my private license was also frustrating my purposes and word got around. Curt Wood stopped me in the hallways of Chadron High School one day in between classes. "Hey," he said. "I heard you flunked the written exam for your private."

"Yeah, what of it?" Though I was known for many things at CHS–clown, athlete, wise guy, and truant–academic scholar was not on the list. Curt, on the other hand, was one of the smartest guys in our class, and he'd already passed his written private exam and was working towards securing his license.

"If you'd like, you can come over to my house," he said. "I can help you pass."

I should have been grateful for his offer, but I mostly felt embarrassed and insecure. I hadn't always been kind to Curt, but here he was, offering to help me. Begrudgingly, I went over to his house. True to his word, Curt helped me prepare, and I passed the test with two points to spare. But beyond that, he taught me how to study. I told him years later that without his help, I probably would have never passed aviation tests, let alone made it through college.

With the written test under my belt, I earned my pilot's license in no time. The closer I got to the mark when I could start earning my Certified Flight Instructor's License (CFI), the more apparent it became that Jim Strang wasn't my biggest fan. He appreciated my grunt work. It wasn't easy to find someone to drive out to the airport each day to sweep the hangar, mow the grassy acreage, drive the firetruck out to change the lightbulbs on the runway, and so forth. He knew I was dependable, that I'd show up on time every time, that I'd work until the job was done right, and I suspect he saw potential in me. But he straight up told me that he would not hire me as a flight instructor for him, even after I earned all my certifications.

It was time for some finagling.

When Jim left for a two-week charter trip to the Bahamas, I took my chance. The wheels were not yet fully retracted in the *Cessna Skymaster* when I cornered the most recently hired flight instructor and told him I'd be flying every single day until my check ride, which I'd already scheduled at the Rapid City Airport. I needed every hour I could get to prepare for this last step that would earn me my CFI. I knew I'd never be able to scrounge up the money to pay for the additional instruction in that short of time, so I charged every dime to Jim's flight school while he was in the Caribbean. I needed Jim on the hook, to give him no other choice but to hire me.

We flew every single day, and I earned my CFI on the same day the *Skymaster* touched ground back in Chadron.

I was out sweeping the hangar when Jim realized I owed him more than $4,000.

It turned out that Jim's voice could boom louder than a jet engine. "How the hell do you plan to pay for this?" he yelled, stomping full-force in my direction.

"Working for you," I said.

"That will take forever." No doubt, Jim was imagining how much physical labor he could get out of me for $4,000.

That's when I showed him my spanking-new CFI. And that's when we agreed that I'd instruct for him until I paid it off.

As a newly minted 18-year-old, I had my first paying job inside of an airplane. And as a brand-new flight instructor, it was amazing that I could now make money doing something that I'd spent so much money doing in the first place.

Despite skipping a great deal of my high school classes, (when else was I supposed to squeeze in all those extra jobs and flight lessons?) they let me graduate. Or maybe they were just ready to get rid of me. At any rate, they signed my diploma. My education continued at the airport, but also moved a block south of my high school to Chadron State College. It turned out that college was an excellent place to hustle new customers for the flight school. My favorite targets were the students whose daddies were paying their way. They had the time and the money to learn to fly.

I soon became Jim's longest employed flight instructor, and I was able to build up about 1000 hours of time. As luck would have it, when the new *Cessna 210 Centurion* arrived, the insurance requirement was 1000 hours to fly the charter as pilot-in-command. The six-seat, high-performance, single-engine machine was a thing of beauty. And, because no one else was available or qualified, I became Chadron's newest charter pilot.

5

Golden Ticket

Two years and $100,000.

They say that's what it takes to become an airline pilot today.

From my experience, it takes more than time and money, but it's a good start. It helps if you love airplanes, the feeling of wielding power beneath your fingertips, and the thrill of escaping into the clouds. Even more important? You need grit. You need the kind of determination to keep going when it's tough, to endure setbacks, to compete at your best even after sleepless nights. Flying the airplane, it turns out, is the easy part.

Working as a flight instructor and a charter pilot at Chadron Municipal Airport helped pay the bills while earning my college degree. But it was a rung on the ladder. The golden ticket on the horizon was my airline transport pilot (ATP) license, the most important piece of paper in my career, which would allow me to finally sit in the cockpits of the lofty jets of the commercial airlines.

I graduated from Chadron State College with a degree in criminal justice and the college's first ever minor in aviation printed on my diploma. The college didn't offer a BS in aviation at the time, so I used what BS I could to finagle the college administrators into awarding me an aeronautics minor. It turns out that BS, along with finagling, are helpful skills in the airline business.

During my time in Chadron, I'd acquired 1200 hours in the sky in addition to every possible license and certification that a pilot could earn at the 'big' airport. To obtain my ATP, I'd need 1500 flying hours and to blow out 23 candles on my birthday cake, the minimum age requirement. I'd grown a bit since my days in Ol' Frank's machine shed, and as a result, I needed a bigger escape. I was still working to fill my frame, which had stretched to just half an inch shy of six-feet. I'd let my hair grow long in high school, but now kept it trimmed, per airline regulations; though try as I might, it never cooperated to lie perfectly flat on top of my head.

I loaded up my '63 Chevy Bel Air. Even my car model's name pointed me to the sky, but all I cared about was that my car was pointed west and with any luck, it would hold together until Phoenix, Arizona. The early 1980s was a boom for the airline industry, thanks in part to the Airline Deregulation Act of 1978 signed into law by President Jimmy Carter. This had the effect of lowering airfare and increasing air travel. As a result, flight schools were popping up all over the country and new airlines were being formed. Rumor had it that the flight schools in Phoenix were hiring instructors. I aimed to be one of them.

Long before the Internet, applying for a job was a face-to-face application with a chief pilot or FBO owner. You had to rely on the mailbox and your copy of Trade-A-Plane to find ads in the Help Wanted section. The increased interest in aviation made pilots a dime a dozen. Getting through the door was half the battle. I'd learned a lesson or two about improving my interviewing skills. This time I came prepared. Instead of bib overalls, I wore a suit. Not only did I wear a shirt, I made sure it was tucked in. I made eye-contact. I shook hands. I landed the job.

If I'd been flying high back in my hometown, the

accelerated flight school in Phoenix was akin to an altitude adjustment. I'd gone from being The Flight Instructor, noted for my young age and impressive resume, to being one of many flight instructors, all the rest younger and with more experience and ratings than me. I felt as if I was always the dumbest guy in the room and had to work harder than everybody else. The hard work I could handle. And believing myself to have such an elevation of improvement before me, set me on a path to obtaining success in an impressively competitive field.

The 1980s were a turbulent time for those who wanted to make a career in the clouds. The economy and massive fluctuations in fuel prices added financial stress to airlines. Labor disputes and striking airline employees disrupted travel, inconveniencing travelers and costing the airlines. Buoyed by government deregulations, airlines expanded their fleets on credit and then sank due to economic uncertainties. Companies bought airplanes, hired pilots, and went broke. Enterprises came and went as fast as airplanes could fly.

While Blondie was topping the charts of the music scene, and hairstyles were growing bigger, bolder, and weirder, I was hopping around the country, grabbing any flying job I could get. One airplane owner asked me if I minded farmwork. I told him I would do whatever it took to fly his airplane.

"Look," he said. "I can find a pilot anywhere, but a good farm worker is hard to find."

To achieve one interview with an airline, applicants could expect to mail out hundreds of resumes. I'd lost track of how many applications I'd filled out, though I had an indent on the side of my middle finger from my pen pressing into it. The path between my house and the mailbox was well trod with my anxious footsteps. Some days, I'd even go to the post office in the morning and see if I could beg for my mail early. If the postman couldn't locate an envelope with my name on it, it felt like the whole day had been wasted. Out of the hundreds of applications, there was seldom a response, and there was no way of knowing whether my resume had even been received. The only thing I could do was go home and fill out more applications. Things were getting desperate enough that I might have accepted a job from a flying monkey, but part of me still held out hope for a letter from Braniff Airlines.

At the beginning of the decade, Braniff International was known as one of the major players in the industry. The company made a name for itself in the 1960s and 1970s with its "End of the Plain Plane" campaign, in which a great deal of money was invested in painting its fleet a variety of colors, from mustard yellow to robin's egg blue, and even emerald-green and orange.

So, when a letter from Braniff Airlines showed up offering class dates, it was like winning the lottery.

When I received my letter, and later my uniform in the mail, I was unaware of the financial strain on the company, or of the mismanagement that had weathered its once-strong position into a barely floating venture. While the vibrant hues of the Braniff planes garnered attention and made them easily recognizable compared to their mostly white counterparts, it did little to help them contend in an overcrowded market.

As I had my uniform tailored, and my emblem properly sewn on, I had only my own success at the forefront of my mind.

We were greeted on our first day of class by the chief pilot, John, who seemed to think failure was more likely than not for Braniff's newest hires. Formidably, he stood before us in full uniform.

"Congratulations," he greeted us. "You are all millionaires. Out of hundreds of applications, 40 of you have been chosen. History will show that less than half of you will complete this program."

With intimidating severity, he handed the first test to the group, which was based on the home study material we'd received in the mail several weeks earlier. I found myself thinking about the single shot .410 shotgun I'd bought as a boy, and how I'd had to teach myself to give the pheasants lead, to mentally calculate the speed of my shot compared to the velocity of a pheasant's wings. There was nothing like the exhilaration I experienced when I took down my first bird, at least until I began the detestable job of cleaning the thing and could barely keep my stomach together. From that time forward, I would feel a great accomplishment each time I shot a bird, but my next thought would always be, "Well shit, now I have to clean this thing."

As I held my pencil over the written exam, the chief pilot's words rang in my ears. "Congratulations," he'd said. "You are all millionaires." But it was apparent to me that this would be no easy bird to butcher.

I filled out the test to the best of my ability and slept poorly that night.

The next day, two of the applicants didn't show up to class. They'd flunked.

From there, we began a week of indoctrination which included company procedures, regulations, and business philosophy. It was incredibly difficult to stay awake, but there was a test at the end of that week, too, so we drank coffee stronger than jet fuel and everyone made it to the next round.

We studied systems with the ground instructors

who were all former mechanics, each with an in-depth knowledge of the *Boeing 727*. They knew everything about the airplane and expected you to know everything, too. In just three weeks, we'd have a written test to prove whether we knew how many pounds of torque it took to hold a certain bolt in place, or if we comprehended the inner workings of advanced magic boxes. For the first time in my life, I experienced sleepless nights, and many of them back-to-back.

Panic set in on the Friday of the test. On Monday morning, we were down another seven students. By this point, the cockiness had been knocked out of all of us with so many classmates failing and not returning. Grit and determination made sure I was one of the students who was still there.

The next phase of testing was what we lovingly called the paper tiger. The term originates from an ancient Chinese philosopher and military strategist, Sun Tzu, who wrote the famous Art of War. I haven't read his book, but from what I understand, the term is used in aviation the same way it was used in the book. A tiger drawn artfully on paper may appear threatening, but in the end it's just paper. Pilots know the importance of understanding all the inner workings of the cockpit and the engineer panel. They know that the hours studying flow-charts, procedures, and the checklists are not in-vain. But at the same time, it's what happens in the real world that matters. When you fly a plane, your life and your passengers' lives depend on your ability to do the right thing at the right time. Whatever you study on paper must translate into operational reality.

This paper tiger phase prepared us for the oral examinations. To this day, I believe oral exams are some of the most difficult. Through experience, I've learned that the key to succeeding and passing an oral test is to only answer the question asked, and to do it in as few words as possible. There's a Bible proverb that seems to agree with me. It says, "The wise store up knowledge, but the mouth of a fool invites ruin." Now I don't always take stock in everything the Bible has to say, but this is one area where me and God can agree.

We were told, "If they ask you what color the line is down the middle of the runway, the answer is white. Don't talk about the green grass or the black tar, because eventually you will talk yourself into an area where you don't know what you are talking about."

On the morning of the orals, the alarm blared at 6 a.m. I reached over and knocked the clock off the bedside table. I'd already seen that clock at midnight, 1:12 a.m., 2:37 a.m., 3:15 a.m., 4:30 a.m., and 5:42 a.m. Each time I'd wake up, I'd stress about the orals, about the sleep I was missing, and then I'd stress about sleeping through my alarm and missing the orals altogether. My only assurance came when I saw all the other applicants later that morning, looking just as disheveled and bleary-eyed.

When it was my turn to enter the test, I crossed my fingers that my brain and mouth would keep up with the rapid-fire questions that were coming at me.

"Explain the position of the surge valve during an emergency operation of the pressurization system."

"The surge valve goes to one-third operation speed."

"Describe what components operate during standby hydraulic system operation."

"The standby hydraulic system usually operates the spoilers in an emergency dissent."

"Would the stabilizer trim be affected if the number two autopilot was inoperative?"

"The stabilizer trim is controlled by the number one autopilot only. Operating with the number two autopilot would require manual trimming."

"Does the APU have fire protection or fire detection?"

"Both if AC power is available. Without AC power, only fire protection."

"What are the limitations on operating the aircraft in the manual version?"

"In the manual version there are speed restrictions."

"When is a second alternate required?"

"Second alternates are required if the weather is at or below minimum two hours before or two hours after your planned arrival."

"You are flying along, and you see this light come on," the instructor pointed to a light on the panel picture. "What are your actions?"

I felt myself switch to autopilot as the questions droned on and on. The training, the studying, and the practice questions that infiltrated my dreams paid off. I felt the questions fairly float out of my mouth as though I'd lost control over my own speech and was watching someone else take the control yoke and maneuver my vocal cords into the correct position.

Following the orals, we were down to 24 applicants.

Simulator training started almost immediately. While I had more than my requisite 1500 hours of flying time, I had never stepped foot inside a simulator. After a few minutes inside the simulator, I felt like I'd never stepped foot inside an airplane.

The first thing I noticed when I entered the simulator building was a distinctive odor, something faint, oily, and chemical. It was a bit like how a tractor smells after a long day's work. I later learned that it was the smell of hydraulic fluid. Simulators are hydraulically operated. I entered the simulator on a gangplank, which was removed shortly after I was in the cockpit. I thought briefly of the pirate stories I'd grown up reading, and it was evident that I was about to be fed to the sharks. Once I was secluded inside, things came fast and furious. I had an idea of what it felt like to be eaten alive. Back then, the simulators didn't feel like an airplane. They were designed to teach procedures. Each pilot had one retry if you failed a lesson, and mine came early in the session.

During the debriefing, the instructor let me know in no uncertain terms that I didn't have a lot of leeway left. Screwing up so early in the training didn't bode well, because I hadn't had a chance to prove myself. The instructor didn't know me from any of the other pilots that walked the gangplank. He couldn't have cared less that I'd never even seen a simulator before that day.

More sleepless nights followed before I got my second chance, knowing that I would not get another one.

During my second time in the simulator, I approached it more like a sophisticated game. I did my best to ignore the inauthentic feel of the machine, and instead allowed my training and knowledge to guide my movements. With the nod of the instructor's head, I knew that I'd live to see another day.

Eventually, only 18 of us met at the gate at Dallas International Airport to do our bounces. Walking down the jetway, as my shoes slapped against the metal, I felt down to the soles of my feet that this was what I had been striving for my entire life. Finally, flying the plane was the easy part.

Each candidate would be required to make three landings and three takeoffs in the actual aircraft. Even though I'd studied the *Boeing 727* for months and flown the simulator, I was still amazed, intimidated, and impressed by the size of this thing. Longer than a basketball court, wider than two school buses, and taller than a three-story building, the behemoth made me feel like an ant scaling the side of a picnic basket. I'd never been so close to such a mechanical giant.

No one wanted to go first. We all stood there, avoiding eye-contact, ears pulsing with the sound of our own blood pumping furiously through our systems. The instructor pointed at me.

"You. Get in the seat."

What happened next was a blur. All I knew is that I was flying a *Boeing 727*! I successfully completed my three landings and takeoffs, and then sat in the back while the other students completed their touching goals. I felt caught in a dream-like sensation, wondering if this was really happening. I looked down at my flight uniform and tugged on my sleeve. *Why was I dressed like this and what the hell was I doing here?* It's like no other feeling, when dreams infiltrate reality.

The last phase of becoming an airline pilot is the IOE, or the Initial Operating Experience. This is a critical phase of training, as it fills the gap between head knowledge and actual airline operations. During this phase, each trainee flies 25 hours with an airline instructor before being released. At around 20 hours, the instructor would tell the chief pilot if we were going to make it or not, but we were still allowed the 25 hours since it was regulation.

Out of my class, 17 made it to the line. I was one of them. I'd achieved the golden ticket.

The next seven months felt like a dream. I couldn't wait to wake up each morning, put on my freshly ironed uniform and get to work. Whenever a pilot joins a new airline, he is put on probation for one year at the very bottom of the seniority list. At the end of the year, he's welcomed into the company as a full-fledged employee, providing his record is satisfactory. I soon discovered the pay was not great at the bottom of the ladder. I made more money driving the Holiday Inn Hotel shuttle van on my days off than I did flying the *727* for Braniff. But I'd keep shuttling people back and forth between their hotels and the airport if it meant that later, I could be back in the airplane, flying those people somewhere farther away.

In 1982, the financial strain on Braniff stretched the company beyond repair, and all operations ceased.

My dream had been grounded.

6

Longer Layovers

Being a pilot is a great job, but a poor career.

I'd imagined that a pilot's life must be a similar experience to an actor's life. Jobs are few and far between, but when you work, you make good money. You just don't work that often; the jobs can be short-lived, and keeping steady employment can be a challenge.

The unpredictability of the pilot's life is just as old as the job itself.

During the earliest decades of aviation, the sky was untouched territory. Pilots were pioneers, and as each daring flier pushed planes farther and higher, the industry evolved. Throughout the 1930s and 1940s, the demand for pilots soared as the possibilities of money-making ventures ignited the imaginations of budding entrepreneurs.

Planes were still in their adolescence when World War II left an enduring mark on the industry. Many able-bodied pilots turned in their commercial uniforms for military regalia, leaving a gap in the civilian sector. Upon their return at the war's end, the airmen were ready to reclaim their commercial flying jobs, and the sudden surplus in pilots led to fierce competition, leaving many unemployed.

The 1960s and 1970s saw some of the largest expansions in the business. Airlines flourished, and the demand for pilots outstripped the stock. This forced the airlines to offer competitive salaries to attract workers, which motivated pilots to jump from carrier to carrier to seek the best opportunities.

Then came the decade of Electric Youth, MTV, neon fashion accessories, and Reaganomics—which sparked a turbulence the airline industry had never seen before. Just as I was entering the career field, the industry saw some of its biggest collapses due to deregulations, economic upheaval, and restructuring. Pilots were hired and fired with equal regularity. New airlines took off and crash-landed.

On a personal note, my own ground operations were expanding. I married in 1983, and we added to our fleet in 1987 and 1989, first with a daughter and then with a son. No longer could I constantly scan the horizon for the next big adventure. Each time I left the runway and ascended into the skies, I knew that back on the ground I had a family who counted on me. And I knew how it felt each time I walked through the front door, greeting my family with the news that once again, I was unemployed.

Driving up the dirt road to our house just outside of Omaha, I felt a mixture of excitement and dread. I hadn't seen my wife and kids for five days, and as much as I wanted to see their smiling faces, I eased off the car's accelerator. I'd been rehearsing stories on the drive from the airport, trying to come up with something to make my news a little more palatable, or at least to make them understand that it wasn't my fault. That I was doing the best I could.

As I pulled into the driveway, I caught a glimpse of my daughter Katie, her nose pressed to the glass on the window that faced our front yard. A second later, Rob was beside her, and I could see his tangled mess of blonde curls as he bounced on the couch, unable to hold his body still.

As soon as I walked through the door, the kids were all over me, and I set my bags down and wrapped them up in my arms. I looked up and saw my wife, Beth, standing in the kitchen. Just by looking at me, she already knew. The dread and stress I carried through the door was something you could sense without words. Once the kids had disentangled their limbs from me, I had to deliver the news. "Well, I'm unemployed again."

The looks on their faces is something permanently and deeply etched into my mind. Though the nation's economic downturns and company restructurings were hardly my fault, I worried doubt would creep into my family's thoughts. *What's wrong with Daddy? and Why can't he keep a job?*

During one memorable occasion, I was informed of my layoff in the plane at altitude. I wondered whether I should advise the passengers that they were now onboard an airplane with three unemployed pilots, and that their connecting flights at their next destination would probably be nonexistent. I felt like a criminal after landing that plane, just trying to escape with what was rightfully mine— a flight bag, suitcase, and sunglasses.

My situation was hardly unique. In fact, I was luckier than many friends. One guy I knew had just signed the mortgage papers on a new home and was laid off a week later. I learned that three pilots committed suicide within one week after their airline went out of business. I've heard countless stories of financial hardships, depression, and families destroyed in this line of work. Early on, I decided that I would never allow a job to become so important to me that I couldn't go on without it. I came to think of my layoffs simply as longer layovers, and I didn't waste my time people-watching or reading magazines. If I had to work a dozen jobs to pay the mortgage, keep food on the table, and make sure the kids had clothes, I'd make the sacrifices. But even while I was stuck on the ground harvesting soybeans for a farmer, my single-minded focus was when and how I could get back into my next airplane.

Harvesting soybeans isn't a euphemism. The list of odd jobs I've worked is as long as it is odd. But I've never believed a college degree and a pilot's license somehow exempted me from doing whatever work is available. If I don't have a job and I need money, then maybe there's a soybean farmer out there who needs help during harvest.

Perhaps my own willingness to dirty my hands has made me less sympathetic for healthy individuals who claim to not be able to find employment. It seems the more accurate statement is they can't find the employment that they want. There are always lawns that need mowed in the summer and walks that need shoveled in the winter. Believe me, I've done both. I've also worked as a handyman, for which I found I had decent talent. I've worked as an estimator for concrete work, and as an estimator for siding on large apartment buildings. I've unloaded trucks, driven trucks, worked on trucks, and sold trucks.

My career as a car salesman only lasted one morning. A young man and his pregnant wife came in looking for a Dodge Charger, but I advised him that they needed to find something much more practical with a baby coming. Once I talked them out of the Charger, they left. The sales manager, who had overheard our conversation, strongly suggested that I find another line of work.

My shortest occupation was for a job in Grand Junction, Colorado. I'd been hired as a consultant to purchase an airplane, with the plan that I'd next be hired to fly it. I was met at the door by a square-shouldered man in a crisp navy-blue suit. A slim coiled transparent tube snaked down from his ear, and his lips were set in a thin line. "Who are you?" was all I got in the way of greeting. It was then that I noticed an FBI pin affixed to his lapel. After momentarily forgetting my own name, I told him who I was and I explained that I was there to start my new job. He grasped the sides of his suit, pulling it open just enough that I could glimpse his sleek black holster that no doubt housed his standard-issued pistol. "I recommend," he said, "that you get back in your car and keep on driving." I thanked him for his time, and then fairly tripped over my own feet on my way back to the car. To this day, I'm not sure what type of a situation I almost walked into. You'd think this would have been a disappointing blow, but an almost-job in aviation was better than no job in aviation.

I once had a short gig with a cattle buyer. I followed him out to the ranch a couple of times and observed while he'd say things to the rancher like, "It's a fine bunch of cattle, but I can only do 36." My boss would go back and forth with the rancher, and he would end up buying them for 38 or 39.

On a busy day, he sent me out to a ranch. The only thing I knew about buying cattle was that my boss only let me go to 36. I talked with the rancher for a while, and finally I said, "It's a fine bunch of cattle, but my boss is only going to let me go 36."

Back with my boss, he asked, "How'd it go?"

"I got them for 36," I said.

"Goddamn, I had to go 39 all day."

That's when I asked my boss the nagging question that had been bothering me. "What exactly does '36' mean?"

Apparently, I'd just bought a herd of cattle for $.36 a pound on the hoof.

Once again, my hard-won skills of finagling and BS proved useful.

Pilots spend a lot of time discussing business ideas. No doubt this is a coping mechanism to soften the blow the next time their airline goes belly-up. One of my ideas was to start a business where I took menus from local restaurants, dropped them off at bars where they only served drinks, and then hired drivers to deliver food to the bars. I was told this was a dumb idea. Though years later, it seemed to work out pretty well for Uber Eats.

Living through cold Nebraska winters gave me another entrepreneurial idea. I could buy used motorcycles at the beginning of the cold season, fix them up, and then sell them for a profit in the spring. In the end, my idea took up a lot of garage space, but didn't yield much profit. I probably could have done a lot better if I'd saved myself the hassle and opened a storage center instead. I learned more from failures than I did from success, namely that if I kept pushing onwards, eventually something would work. But if I quit, there'd be nothing to show for it. I started and sold a computer business. I owned and operated a tree trimming business. I launched a security business with a good friend of mine, Mark Sundermeier. My son and I opened a firewood business and a lawn care business. We've bought houses, fixed them up, and turned them into rental properties.

One pilot I knew started a junkyard and became a millionaire. Several left flying altogether and became lawyers or engineers, or something more likely to bring in steady income. Another pilot, while on furlough, was watching workers put up metal buildings and he noticed that the screws they used were shining in the sunshine. He asked the contractor why they didn't use painted screws. "Because," the contractor said, "there's no such thing as a painted screw." The pilot went home that day and started painting screws in his garage. He eventually bought a warehouse and made quite a profit selling painted screws. We gave him the nickname "Screwy."

It's impossible to remember all the names and all

the stories. I've known pilots who sold everything they owned on furlough, just to hang in there until the next flying job. I've met more pilots than I care to admit, whose financial hardships and insecure employment led to divorce and broken families. Almost every pilot I've ever met will tell you that they weren't in the business for the money. There's a love of aviation that draws them back, something I'm not yet able to fully explain. I know I'm not the only pilot who will do whatever it takes to get back into the sky.

Let's be honest. I've been envious of the individual who can hold the same job for 35 years, live in the same house, and get to work by the same route every day. But I have as much sorrow for that person as I have envy, because what in the world is that person going to write a book about?

7

Furloughed, Fired, or ...

As a 14-year-old, I was willing to break a few laws to get closer to my dream–trespassing and occasional truancy, to start. Once I had access to Ol' Frank's machine shed, I was willing to work harder than two or three 14-year-olds combined to scrounge together $12 each week to fly. At the time, I'd have been willing to open a vein if it meant I could go up into that vast Nebraska sky. From up there, I could almost see past the horizon, but I never saw a future where flying wouldn't bring me joy. But somehow, it became a job.

I remember reading about the true story of Daniel "Rudy" Ruettiger's life, which was later made into the 1993 movie, *Rudy*. The inspirational sports biography follows Rudy Ruettiger as he chased his goal of becoming a college football player. He faced so many obstacles, even his family discouraged him from pursuing such an unrealistic ambition. Despite not having the talent or the physicality to be a football player, Rudy remained undeterred; through sheer perseverance and drive, finally earned a spot on the Notre Dame football team. The obvious moral is, don't give up. Whatever you want is within your grasp. This is all warm and fuzzy, but what caught my attention was that in the immediate years after achieving his goal, Rudy's life was hard. He seemed lost. He no longer had a clear direction driving him forward.

I could relate. There were days encapsulated within the years of layoffs, starting over, and circling Help Wanted ads, that I felt like I needed a map to navigate the once-clear runway in front of me. A nagging question kept encroaching my thoughts. *Why did I learn to fly in the first place?*

The simple answer was because it was fun. I wanted to explore the world in those beautiful machines, escape into the clouds, and experience adventure. Suppressing my emotions, a well-honed family trait, had always worked well enough to get me through tough spots in life. The sky was my place of escape. The thrill of adventure and the euphoria of chasing a dream was enough to distract me from the lingering, persistent questions. But this question kept coming back, louder and louder, like the roar of a jet engine, impossible to subdue. Wasn't this supposed to be fun?

Dwindling bank accounts.

Starting over at the bottom, airline after airline.

Watching friends with steady jobs buy boats and newer houses with bigger garages.

But I always came back to a second question. *What else could I do that would be as fun as flying an airplane?* The delight of taking off and soaring skyward had not diminished for me. It was still enjoyable fun. But everything between the takeoffs and landings became a job, a truly unpleasant one.

The vicious cycle of reaching the top and starting over again drains a person over time. Those up and down plummets are fun if you like roller coasters, but the feeling in the pit of your stomach when it's your career that's taking a plunge is anything but a thrill. Receiving a furlough as an experienced captain, only to be hired by another airline as a brand-new copilot with no seniority is a rough landing if there ever was one.

I still feel sorry for the captain who received the blunt end of my frustration one evening over dinner during a layover in LaGuardia. I'd recently been hired as his lowly copilot, despite my years of experience, my recent high ranking with a previous airline, and with tens of thousands of hours of flight time to my credit. We were within walking distance to our hotel for the evening, and after passing several family-style restaurants, we settled into a booth of an establishment with a spiral-bound menu and a galaxy of gastronomic choices.

I searched the menu for something priced lower than my per diem, and settled on a gyro platter and a glass of water. I watched with some envy as the captain ordered a glass of wine and a large ribeye steak. When the food arrived, I couldn't help but notice how his knife seemed to slip through the meat on its own accord; it was that tender.

"It must be nice to have that kind of money to eat on," I said. "With probation pay, I can barely afford to wipe my butt. Remind me to steal some toilet paper from the hotel before I leave tomorrow."

I expected a chuckle from across the table, but instead the captain slowly chewed his steak, his thick brows shadowing his eyes. He swallowed, sipped from his wine glass, and then looked straight at me. "Well Son, you have to pay your dues in this business."

The tzatziki from the gyro platter turned rancid on my tongue.

"What the hell would you know about paying dues?" I asked him.

Here was a man who'd managed to squeak through most of the industry's turnovers. Everything in his career had gone well for him and he was about to retire. He blotted his shiny wine-soaked upper lip with his napkin. "I've been here almost 30 years. I had to start at the bottom also."

"I've started at the bottom seven times," I said.

"Well, Son—"

"Let's talk dues. I've spent more time than you in a *Boeing*. I have experience in both seats and I've been a check airman. I have a college degree and I'm not over-weight, so when there's an emergency, I'm not going to get my fat ass jammed into the exit window. Based on the last couple of days of observing you fly, I'd judge you weak at best, and honestly I don't know how you made it through the last session of training." I felt myself shaking, my voice getting louder. I could feel people's eyes on us from across the restaurant, but I couldn't rein myself in. "Your arrogance sickens me. But maybe you aren't arrogant. Maybe you're just ignorant. But if you don't know what the hell you're talking about, it would behoove you to keep your mouth shut."

"Well, Son—"

"Kiss my ass, I'm moving to another table."

I don't know whatever became of him, but I have a feeling he didn't forget me or the dinner that night. But if I had a chance to see him again, I would apologize to him, even knowing how wrong and thoughtless I still believe that he was.

Just prior to that dinner experience, I'd attended the funeral of my close friend and fellow pilot, Bruce Clark. His plane crashed in a crop-dusting accident. At his memorial service, someone said, "At least he died doing what he loved."

To this day, when I hear someone use that justification, it cuts deep. I think I know why.

Bruce died trying to support his family. Whether or not he enjoyed what he was doing is probably insignificant at this point. The only reason he'd been in a crop-dusting plane is because he'd been furloughed from his airline job.

He and I had both been dropped to the bottom of the seniority list, a place where neither one of us felt like we belonged. We were both forced to take other jobs, find work wherever we could find it, and we did.

Like any business, when an airline sees the writing on the wall, they must start stuffing the sausages with sawdust, saving money in any way possible, and the most common way for them to do this is to furlough pilots. This way they can dangle their pilots at the end of the line and reel them in, if and when their financial situation reverses. The pilots are still technically a part of the airline, but no paychecks are coming their way. The word, 'furlough,' has always had a negative connotation for me. I've always said, "furloughed, fired, or fucked, all the same in the airline business."

A furloughed pilot is a bit like an airplane without wings. Sure, you could turn the airplane into an oversized storage unit or an unwieldy bus, but at the end of the day you've taken away its purpose. You've grounded what was destined to fly.

Pilots lucky enough to not be furloughed might see their luck run out soon enough. These pilots were often scheduled to work to their legal limits each month, meaning they would have flown the maximum number of hours allowed by the FAA. Once those hours were met, the pilots knew they'd need to start seeking new employment, because more likely than not, the rest of their contract would not be honored.

A long enough furlough can take your mind down some interesting paths. I can remember asking my friend how hard it was to become a mortician. He told me I just needed 18 months of school in San Francisco, and he'd hire me on the spot. When I read an article about the salaries of experienced garbage men in New York City, I won't say I wasn't tempted. In college, I took a class on arson investigation, which seemed like an interesting line of work to fall back on, but I never figured out how to break into that profession.

I'd often fall back to my tree business during furloughs. One of my customers had a large job, and I worked for him on and off for about three weeks. I spoke with him on occasion. I treated him like a customer, and he treated me like a tree man. One day at Midway Airport in Chicago, I saw him staring at me. I was in my airline uniform, waiting at the gate for my plane to arrive so I could start my day. I recognized him right away. He kept staring at me but would glance away quickly if our eyes met. It was obvious to me why I'd summoned his interest. At last, curiosity got the best of him, and he made his way over to me. "Excuse me, Captain," he said. "But do I know you?"

I answered politely, "Yes you do. I'm your tree man."

A look of bewilderment crossed his face, "But ..." he stammered. "Why are you here? And why are you dressed like that?"

I just shrugged under the shoulder pads of my captain's uniform, "I dabble in several things when there's no trees to cut down."

Having owned a few businesses, I know a little something about offering a person a job. Instantaneously, you see their body language shift. Something changes in their facial expression. I've always thought it was poetic. Regardless of what that job is, you can see that person believes their life is about to change for the better. It's necessary to feel wanted. I don't have the psychological training to explain it, but a person requires a challenge and a reason to believe that their life means something. It might be a sad commentary on humanity, but many people get that feeling from being offered a job.

I've had more than my fair share of experiences in

accepting a job, and the feeling of reaching across the table to shake someone's hand never changes. Even when I knew that it meant starting back at square one in the six-to-eight-week training course required of all new hires, my mind just accepted that it was time to go to work, and this was just part of the profession that I'd chosen.

Bitterness and anger over the many pitfalls of my career used to be a regular part of my diet, but the mind has an uncanny ability to forget the bad and only remember the good as the years pass by. These days, I don't even feel like I have a job anymore. It feels more like a hobby that pays well.

Back when I flew on reserve, the sound of a ringing phone in the middle of the night would send dread up my spine. While your body begs for more sleep, your brain goes on high alert, engulfed in wondering where you might be going, and why the phone is ringing in a dark crash pad. Today I look forward to phone calls. When I look down and see that my boss is calling, I feel eager and enthusiastic because we'll be back in the sky soon. On occasion, I will even call him with a suggestion of where we should fly next.

One day he asked me, "Where do you want to go?"

"Well," I said, "that's a question I've never been asked in my entire career as a pilot."

Given a choice, I'd probably fly to Nashville to visit my daughter and grandkids. I honestly believe we will take that trip before the insurance companies tell me I'm too old to fly, even knowing it costs my boss around six grand an hour to operate his *Falcon 50*.

8

Crash Pad Chronicles

Before I even walked through the door, I could smell garlic and red pepper flakes. The sound of shrimp sizzling in the pan was the kind of welcome home I'd been hoping for. But it wasn't my wife standing over the stove, and in the strictest technicalities, it wasn't really my home. Instead, it was my friend Jeremy who wielded the spatula; and the abode was an apartment in Chicago, which I shared with eight to ten of my fellow pilots.

"I've been peeling shrimp for five hours," Jeremy said, by way of greeting. "I just bought these on the coast."

Dinner was delicious. Fresh-caught shrimp in the middle of the country is a luxury to most, but for a group of pilots, your food options are not limited to what can be bought in a grocery store. We'd had live lobsters on numerous occasions, farm-fresh corn in the middle of winter, oranges straight from a tree in California, and decadent delicacies from all around the country.

At the Chicago crash pad, we all thought of ourselves as professional chefs, and on the days we arrived early enough in the afternoon, we took turns preparing "crash pad cuisine," some of the best and worst meals I've ever had. Despite our inflated sense of culinary prowess, not everyone shared the same skills in the kitchen. Sometimes dinner was simply "crash pad chili," which was basically a can of beans warmed up in a pan and served with a lot of pepper.

You'd think that pilots would avoid the word 'crash' at all costs. At least that is the desperate wish of the first-time flier sitting back in economy seat 22B. And yet, at the end of the day, many pilots and crew return to their 'crash pad' to recharge for the next leg of their journey.

Unlike your average accountant, who likely walks out of their front door each morning, drives to an office building, sits at a stationary desk, and then returns home at the end of the day, a pilot's commute can be somewhat more convoluted.

In fact, most pilots don't even live in the same town as their hub airport. Since frequent layoffs are part of the landscape, it's not feasible for a pilot to pack up and move across the country each time a new job becomes available. It's hard enough to walk through the door and tell your family that you are unemployed again. Imagine telling your kids that they no longer have the same house, the same school, or the same friends. Or try telling your spouse that she'll need to terminate her established career and follow you to the next airport. These are not realistic scenarios, or at least they weren't for me.

If, like me, you live in Omaha, Nebraska, and your next airline job is in Chicago, Illinois, you simply adjust your commute. For many airline employees, a crash pad is the answer. Featuring two or three bedrooms stocked full of bunk beds, a bathroom, kitchen, and a few couches where you can feel at home while away from your family, these apartments are usually rented on the cheap and help lessen the nightmare of commuting.

Being a commuter in the airline industry is like having a part-time job with no pay. Somewhere between my takeoffs and landings, my communications with air traffic control, and the announcements I made to my passengers,

I needed to be asking myself *How am I going to get back home?*

You'd think nothing would be easier for someone who works in the travel industry than to find a way home, but several factors have complicated the equation. Most people are familiar with jump seats and assume that pilots can hop on one any time they like. Jump seats, located in the flight deck, can be folded down when needed. They are typically reserved for authorized personnel, and most often utilized by pilots, but the easy accessibility of jump seats for pilots is a misconception.

Each location has its unique challenges, and though I can't speak to all of them, I can attest to what it's like living in Omaha. We have the College World Series each summer, Warren Buffet's annual meeting, the United States Olympic Team Trials for Swimming, the U.S. Senior Golf Open Championship, and multiple other events that fill up airplanes and make it difficult for a pilot to get a jump seat home.

For several years after the September 11, 2001, terrorist attacks, pilots weren't even allowed to use the jump seats. The government revoked jump seat privileges for pilots, further limiting our abilities to commute home. Instead, pilots were required to fly standby with no priority over other passengers. To this day, I wonder how many congressmen, senators, judges, lawyers, doctors, and merchants lost their ride to work in the interest of public safety. In the last two decades, security measures have progressed, and some jump seat privileges have been reinstated, but the ability to use these seats remains under tight-fisted control.

Long story short, a pilot's commute can be a pain in the ass.

A pilot's crash pad goes a long way in taking the sting out of commuting, in part because of the community formed with fellow coworkers. While the make-up of each pad is different, I always roomed with a bunch of guys; and beyond shared space, we bonded over meals, experiences, stories, and once, over a breast implant. More on that later.

Over the course of my career, I've had crash pads in Indianapolis, Indiana; Colorado Springs and Denver, Colorado; Gulfport, Mississippi; Miami and Destin, Florida; Las Vegas, Nevada; and in New York, New York. The crash pad I kept the longest was the one in Chicago, near Midway. At the time I had one of the steadiest flying jobs of my career working for American Trans Air. Arriving at the crash pad was never uneventful. You didn't know until you turned the key in the lock whether you'd have the place to yourself, or whether ten guys would be crammed inside an apartment that comfortably slept five. Weather, technical difficulties, aircraft maintenance, air traffic control delays, and passenger delays make unpredictability the most predictable thing in a pilot's life. I used to tell my mom when making visits back home, "I'll be there when I walk through the door." Take one erratic schedule times ten, and you'll get some idea of what crash pad life is like.

There aren't necessarily assigned chores in a crash pad, but it's understood that everyone cleans up after themselves, pays their share of the rent, and does their part to keep the place running. We'd take turns cooking as schedules allowed, though there were often takeout containers in the trash or leftovers that may or may not be up for grabs. The rules with food are unique to each crash pad. Sometimes the food becomes a community resource once it's put into the cupboards or fridge, though other pilots are a bit more exclusive in their food consumption. You haven't seen everything until you've seen someone put a padlock on a Tupperware container. For the record, I've seen everything.

Living with fellow pilots brings a whole new level of

intimacy amongst coworkers. Sharing kitchen space, bath-rooms, and bunkrooms gives deeper insights into each other's lives than a typical office environment. Phenome-nal friendships can be born out of these close living quar-ters; however, you get to know some people much more than you ever wanted. Other personalities are quiet, unas-suming, but well-worth the effort of getting to know. One such man was a humble older gentleman who was in my new-hire class at ATA and moved into our crash pad. His name was Harold Icke, and while he didn't divulge his every thought, we enjoyed having him around.

During the first day of the new hire class, all the stu-dents were required to stand up, tell who they were, and share their past flying experiences. Harold stood. "I guess I'm kind of a low-time man around here. I'm retired Air Force."

It wasn't until Dan Shipner, our crash pad's self-proclaimed aviation history buff, was reading *The Rescue of Bat 21* by Darrel D. Whitcomb, that we discovered Har-old Icke's identity. It turned out that the modest gentle-man who'd been living among us, was none other than Col. Harold Icke, a decorated war veteran. Not only was he a retired member of the United States Air Force, but Harold was one of the forward air control pilots who was instru-mental in the rescue operation of Lt. Col. Iceal "Gene" E. Hambleton during the Vietnam War. In April of 1972, Hambelton, an Air Force navigator, was shot down and stranded behind enemy lines. The harrowing tale of Ham-bleton's successful rescue was made into the 1988 action movie *Bat*21*, starring Gene Hackman and Danny Glover. We later realized that when Harold said he "was a low-time man," that the majority of his flight hours were combat time. One hour of combat flight is probably worth more than 200 hours of straight and level flying.

When we confronted Harold about being a national

war hero, he just said, "There were a lot of people involved. It wasn't just me." I've since watched a documentary about Harold on YouTube, and he's as humble on camera as he is in real life. I now keep track of him on Facebook, and he's traveling the world, sampling beers, and playing golf. Well-deserved, Harold.

In contrast to Harold, we also lived with a guy that I'll call Bill. Bill liked to stretch out the phone cord in the apartment, shouting into the mouthpiece, pretending he was running a large corporation, trying to impress us. In addition to the obviously phony phone conversations, he'd leave advanced-looking mathematical formulas lying around the apartment, goading us to ask him about them. Unfortunately for Bill, one of the pilots in our crash pad had majored in math in college, and said the papers were filled with numerical gibberish.

Bill would run his mouth at just about every opportunity, and none of us could put up with him for very long. Bruce Clark, probably my closest friend in the crash pad, had a supernaturally calm demeanor. He was one of those guys who could get along with anyone, and he was even nice to Bill. One particular afternoon, Bruce was watching the Red Sox play on television. If he hadn't become a pilot, Bruce probably would have been a baseball coach. He loved the Red Sox, and even played on their farm team for two years. He liked to remind me that no matter how good I got in the batting cage, I couldn't hit pitches off him. He could throw a curveball at my head, causing me to jump out of the way as the ball crossed the strike zone.

Though the Red Sox game was obviously in full swing, Bill walked into the living room and changed the channel to an Apollo One documentary. We all tensed up a bit, watching Bill sink back into the couch, oblivious to what an ass he was being. Bruce, a devout Mormon who didn't drink, cuss, or even eat junk food, sat quietly on the couch, and didn't say a word.

The documentary was all about the fire that killed Gus Grissom, Ed White, and Roger B. Chaffee during a pre-launch test on January 27, 1967. "Can you believe this stuff?" Bill said. "All these so-called scientists and they couldn't even spot such a simple mistake. When I was in junior high, I wrote a letter to NASA and explained the fire danger because of the small gauge wire they were using in the construction of the space capsule." Bill told a lot of stories which featured him as the hero, how he could've saved the day in this situation or that situation, but that no one had listened to him. Had any of us been interested in watching the documentary, we wouldn't have been able to hear it over the constant droning of Bill's vocal cords.

"Shut the fuck up, Bill," Bruce said, causing us all to simultaneously drop our mouths open in both shock and merriment.

"Now wait a minute," Bill yammered on. "You've got to understand the situation of a space capsule full of pure oxygen and that tiny little spark, all the flammable—"

"I guess you didn't understand me," Bruce said. "I said, shut the fuck up."

For once, Bill closed his mouth. Someone got up and changed the channel back to the Red Sox game.

I don't know this for sure, but I'd be willing to gamble that at some point, Bruce apologized to Bill when nobody else was around. That's the type of guy he was. I just remember looking at Bruce after the Red Sox game was back on the television. He looked right back at me. Without words, we communicated that it was high time someone had put a stopper in Bill's diatribes.

After taxiing an airplane into a pole on two consecutive occasions, Bill's job, and his presence in our crash pad, disappeared. I'm not saying that Bill ever padlocked his Tupperware, but I'm also not saying he didn't.

Another crash pad buddy, just a kid and new to the airline, was bragging one evening about his flight-attendant girlfriend.

"I'm telling you, Don, it was the best $3000 I ever spent."

"Was it a two-for-one special, or did you spring for both?"

The kid laughed. "That's the price for both of them. Have you ever seen a pair of fake tits?"

"I've seen plenty of movies."

"Wait, you've never seen any in real life?"

I shrugged, but admitted that I had never seen or touched an artificial breast.

"Have you even lived? Listen, Lucinda's picking me up in about 15 minutes for our date. You'll have to check them out."

When we heard the rap on the door, the kid jumped over the back of the couch, and I could hear the murmur of voices as he invited her inside. I barely had time to notice her breasts, because she was basically wearing denim underwear in place of shorts and her legs stretched about a mile long.

I lifted my hand in greeting.

"Don is lacking in life experiences," the kid said, filling her in on our conversation. She shrugged, walked over to me, and raised her shirt. "Go ahead, touch 'em."

I did and they left. I never saw her again or had a chance to thank her.

Interesting sidenote . . . Over the course of my life, more people have asked me about what the breast felt like than stories about Harold Icke. This may be one indication something is wrong with our country.

One more interesting sidenote . . . they were very firm. Apparently, she'd selected the permanently hard nipple option.

Crash pads can come and go just as quickly as airliner jobs. The apartment we shared in Chicago was sold without warning, and we had to find a new place–and quickly. Furthermore, the landlord told us that all the furniture had to be out ASAP. None of us had trucks, since Chicago wasn't our permanent residence; so we got a bid to see how much it would cost to get the furniture moved. When we found out it was going to be more than $700, we needed a plan B.

Bob Hemingway and I were the only ones available to move the furniture since everyone else was either at home or flying. The only tools at our disposal were our muscles and our brains. We put both to good use. Together, we heaved the furniture out to the front yard. Then we hung a hand-made sign on the front of it that said, "Do not steal." Within the hour, all the furniture was gone.

Our next stop was a furniture store that was within walking distance. We cleared our old crash pad, but now we needed furniture for the new apartment. We found a floor sample of a couch, a La-Z-Boy, and a loveseat, all ensconced in what used to be white leather, but had turned dingy gray, streaked with customer fingerprints. It looked so bad that the manager sold the whole lot to us and delivered it to our new dwelling place for $100. After a decent amount of elbow grease, we were living in high cotton again.

Since crash pads are located in close proximity to major airports, it's not uncommon for a neighborhood to house multiple crash pads. Once in a while, several crash pads will decide to have a block party. Everyone is invited, and sometimes it's so much fun that the police show up. We later learned that in order to have a block party in Chicago, you had to apply for a block party permit.

It seems like each crash pad acquires its own reputation. Some are party places. Others are known for old men who just like to sleep. There was even one that was famous for its flight attendants who liked to keep their window shades open when they changed out of their uniforms.

Our crash pad was pretty much old married men, but I'm not saying that we didn't leave our window shades open from time to time.

Airlines come and go, and when they go, all the employees are unceremoniously removed from the property and left out on the curb to see who'll take them next.

American Trans Air filed for Chapter 11 bankruptcy protection on April 2, 2008. On April 3, 2008, the company basically changed course mid-flight and immediately ceased all operations. This shocking decision not only significantly impacted all the pilots who lost their jobs that day, but it also canceled all flights, leaving passengers stranded across the contiguous United States, in Hawaii, and around the globe.

For me, and for the men I had shared space with over the last several years, it was a crash landing. Our Chicago pad disbanded. We took down each other's home phone numbers. Promised we'd stay in touch. Assumed that we'd see each other again soon. But phone numbers changed. We lost track of who went where. And the truth was, staying in touch wasn't high on the priority list compared to finding new jobs and feeding our families. Had this happened in the time of social media, things might have been different; but instead I'm left with a question that has plagued me throughout my career. Where are all those good friends that I spent so much time with? Not having an answer for that question is perhaps the saddest part of all.

When the job ends, you lose touch with the people who you so recently cooked meals with, shared stories with, and with whom you fondled the occasional breast.

When ATA went bankrupt, we didn't even have the heart to carry the furniture out to the curb. We packed our personal belongings and walked out of the apartment in the dark of night. I remember the white furniture gleaming in the moonlight through the unshaded windows. We hoped the next occupants would like it as much as we did. It's a sad and lonely feeling, locking the door of an apartment behind you, knowing that you'll never quite recreate the camaraderie you found. The last time I saw my dear friend, Bruce Clark, was in the dark that night as we were leaving the crash pad.

"Well, what's next?" I asked him as we took our final descent down the apartment stairs.

"You know," Bruce said. "Same as always, I might take on some seasonal work until things come through. You?"

"I'll start sending out applications tomorrow and go back to tree trimming."

"Take care of yourself, Ozzie. Hope to see you up there soon," he pointed skywards.

"Yeah man, see you on the other side."

We figured we'd meet up again soon, but the next time I saw him was at his funeral. He died in a crash doing seasonal work in a crop-dusting accident.

9

Above the Fallen Towers

I'd never flown a plane over anything like it.

Clouds of thick, white smoke clung to the air over open mouthed-holes choking on the rubble of fallen buildings. It was as though a part of New York City had been swallowed by a beast, chewed, and spewed into a blackened mess. The towers of the World Trade Center, which had always saluted passing planes, now bowed low, flames smoldering weeks later. This was a fire that would burn for 99 days, but the heat of those embers would spread throughout the airline industry, scorching all that we had known before.

On September 8, 2001, I flew out of Logan International Airport in Boston. My schedule that month took me on a route between Boston, Los Angeles, Chicago, and Newark. As I pushed back from the gate that day, I could have never foreseen that in just three days, in the gate right next to mine, a hijacker would board United Airlines Flight 175 and fly a *Boeing 757* into the South Tower of the World Trade Center, forever changing the skyline and the entire landscape of aviation.

In the weeks following the September 11, 2001, terrorist attacks, airports became ghost towns. Our airline was one of the first allowed back into Newark Liberty International. My feet echoed down the long, deserted terminals, hardly ever passing another human. And when you did cross paths with someone, it was evident they were flying because they had no choice. They wore haunted facial expressions, their eyes darkened with fear, despair, and bewilderment.

The reflection in my mirror was much the same. In the month after the attacks, I not only flew over the blazing wreckage of NYC, but when I was scheduled to fly to Reagan National Airport in D.C., I walked the few miles between my hotel and the Pentagon, witnessing the aftermath firsthand. The whole thing was repulsive. Those beautiful planes, incredible feats of engineering and human ingenuity, were turned into bombs.

Aviation is not for people looking for a steady income. It's not a career path for someone hoping to hold the same job until retirement. It's not a great job choice if you want to tuck your kids into bed each night and be there to celebrate all the holidays with them. There's something much deeper that draws people like me into this field. It's that strange and unexplainable love for those powerful machines, the feeling of freedom and escape as you rise above the clouds and just for a while, the ground goes white beneath you. This is a career for those 14-year-old kids who sneak into machine sheds, just for the chance to be close enough to an airplane that they can imagine themselves in a different life and start to dream.

The celebrated brother duo, inventors of the airplane, Orville and Wilbur Wright, were famously hesitant to sell their aircraft to the military for reconnaissance. Their interests focused on commercial and civilian purposes, and they were concerned that their invention of upward exploration would instead be turned into a destructive force in warfare. Their opinions changed over time, perhaps in part to the financial upswing that a military contract could bring, and they licensed and sold their airplanes to various governments, including the U.S. Military.

On 9/11, I witnessed what could happen when airplanes were turned into weapons.

If you have the desire to hear an incredibly emotional discussion, somehow put yourself in the middle of a group of pilots who feel the freedom to have an open conversation. Eventually, the subject of 9/11 will rear its ugly head, and you'll hear our lamentations about living in a society that put political correctness above the safety of American citizens. Like most pilots, even after all these years, I am still disgusted about how our industry succumbed to lax standards. We dedicated ourselves to this business, then watched it crumble in front of our eyes. I believe the terrorists knew they could get people into the cockpit of a major airline, given the de-emphasis on knowledge, skill, and experience requirements for pilots.

In the weeks and months following the attacks, I spent more time talking with passengers than ever before. Some were scared, some were depressed, and some were filled with rage. One particular gentleman told me that he'd always considered himself a pacifist. "But after watching those towers fall," he said, "I want revenge, I want carnage." He wondered aloud if he was too old to join the military.

I was too young for Vietnam, and too old for Desert Storm, but I could relate to the frenzy that thundered in that passenger's eyes. I remember in grade school and high school seeing young men in wheelchairs, dealing with severe wartime injuries. Few things have made my blood boil more than innocent lives lost for political gain. The loss and devastation of the 9/11 terrorist attacks left me angrier than almost anything else ever had.

Decades before 9/11, pilots were already receiving 'Hijack Training,' sometimes called 'Cooperation Training' or 'The Common Strategy.' This training was necessitated by the alarming number of planes hijacked in the 1960s and 1970s. In the height of that era, it's estimated that at least one plane was hijacked every five days. During these hundreds of hijackings, pilots were forced to redirect their flights to other countries, most commonly Cuba. Most airlines at the time even carried approach plates for Cuba in case of a hijacking.

During those years, thousands of passengers found themselves unexpectedly in Cuba, but fortunately, few were ever harmed. Most of the hijackers were politically motivated, and the diverted planes were a way to draw attention to their political and social issues, often stemming from the turbulent governmental climates of the Middle East and other regions during that era. Cuba's policy of offering asylum to hijackers made it a popular destination.

Other planes were hijacked over money.

Arthur Gates Barkley ended up in a psychiatric ward after his attempted hijacking of a plane out of Dulles International Airport in 1970. He'd been in a heated dispute with the IRS over a charge of $417.78 in back taxes, and figured commandeering TWA Flight 486 was a reasonable plan of action. When the plane landed, the FBI tricked Barkley with a bag of fake money. Agents jumped on him, but not before he shot one of the pilots, who mercifully survived.

D.B. Cooper became a wanted man in 1971. After hijacking a plane and demanding $200,000 in ransom money, he made a dramatic escape, jumping out of the plane with his money and a parachute. He was never heard from again, and the case is still considered one of the great unsolved mysteries.

Learning to deal with hijackers became a regular part of the recurrent training required for airline pilots. Some pilots, depending on their position, receive recurrent training as much as every three months. Some quick addition tells me that I've had as much classroom training as anyone with a PhD. My stepfather used to say he had a PhD. He said it stood for post hole digger.

The hijack training we received was about the equivalent of post hole digging, for all the good it did on an airplane. It was written and produced by ignorant government officials whose knowledge of aviation security could be summed up in a single clod of dirt. For more than 25 years, most of us complained about this training. I know many pilots who wrote letters, formed committees, and tried to lobby congressmen with pleas to change the training into something more realistic and effective.

The training went something like this: In the event of a hijacking situation, the pilot, as the person in command, was to become subservient, agreeable, and do whatever they could to make the hijacker feel relaxed and comfortable before finally diverting the plane to the destination of the hijacker's choice. The protocol didn't necessarily require us to prepare a complimentary cocktail for our hostile guest, but it might as well have. The purpose behind this approach was to prioritize the safety of the passengers and crew, thereby avoiding outright conflict. This approach was rooted in the belief that it was better to send a plane to Cuba where passengers could at least enjoy some Havana nightlife, pristine beaches, and purchase a few illegal cigars, rather than escalate the situation through resistance.

My fellow pilots and I would sit in the back of the classroom during these enlightened lectures and think to ourselves, *Bullshit.*

By the time we were receiving this training, the hijacking era had ended. The end of the Cold War, which brought about international agreements and increased law enforcement cooperation, had all but ended these politically motivated airplane takeovers. Despite new technologies and new political unrest in new parts of the world, we received the same stagnant instructions for decades.

On September 11, 2001, I believe most of the pilots were acting and performing exactly how they were trained. But the training failed. The training allowed terrorists to reroute airplanes, not to the tropical island of Cuba, but into buildings and fields. The atrocities performed that day, while complex and multifaceted, highlighted what pilots had been saying for years. The safety measures and training we received were outdated and foolish.

Since the attacks, policies have changed regarding pilot training. The cockpit is now secured and locked during flights. The previous passive cooperation approach has been replaced with active resistance. Some good steps have been taken in the name of security. But some post-9/11 decisions have been steps in the wrong direction. Take, for instance, the jump seat privileges that were revoked for pilots after the attacks. Due to ill-informed regulations that were put into place by government officials rather than by aviation experts, pilots were removed from jump seats and forced to fly standby. Wouldn't it make more sense to fill the flight deck with additional individuals who were trained to band together and fight off hijackers or terrorists? Instead, those jump seats were left empty; and pilots, once the heroes of the sky, were under added scrutiny.

The creation of the Transportation Security Administration (TSA) following the 9/11 attacks was also put in place to protect pilots and passengers, but it's been called a 'Security Theater,' for good reason. The program was signed into law by President George W. Bush in November of 2001, and has been a source of debate among both passengers and pilots about its effectiveness and efficiency. The agency replaced former private security screening contractors in an attempt to standardize security procedures, but from my experience, the standard of quality is low.

While the TSA claims to comprehensively train its employees, I've witnessed a lack of adequate training on many occasions. To me, it's the same old government story, putting very poorly trained personnel in positions of authority. I don't blame the workers; I blame the policies that sent them to work without the needed skill set. The TSA agents no doubt passed the several-week-training course required, but I question whether it was the right training to begin with.

Following the September 11 attacks, I underwent specialized education and was deputized as a Federal Flight Deck Officer, which authorized me to carry and use a firearm as part of the flight crew on a commercial aircraft. It seems to me there is a certain level of ignorance associated with a TSA agent digging through your suitcase looking for fingernail clippers when you are carrying a gun. I can't tell you how many times that happened.

I once asked a TSA agent, "What are you looking for? I can help you find it."

She said, "I'm looking for something that will allow you to take command of an airplane."

Of course, I was in full uniform, surrounded by my crew at the time. I said, "As soon as you're done with me, I plan to take command of an airplane."

Critics have argued that the TSA is slow to adapt to emerging threats, that employees have been lackadaisical in following procedures while conducting screenings, that procedures are inconsistent from airport to airport, and that some measures, such as removing shoes or limiting liquids, may not be effective in preventing certain types of threats.

My sister's kid had her nerf gun confiscated in a TSA line. In that same security screening, the agents overlooked a kitchen knife that my sister forgot was in her purse. I'm not sure it makes sense that they allow long knitting needles through security, but then they worry about how much your toothpaste weighs.

Sometimes I feel like I just can't shake my head hard enough.

The Administrators of both the TSA and FAA are politically appointed positions by the President of the United States. I'm not holding my breath, but I'd have a few suggestions if my name was drawn out of a hat. For one, I'd increase antiterrorist and security training. I would increase the requirements for TSA agents. I'd reduce the TSA and increase the Air Marshall program. And I know it's a nasty word, but I'd make sure we were profiling. And then profile what we profiled. In safety related issues, where people's lives depend on people performing professionally, we have to start hiring competent people and stop hiring people to just fill a role. In my opinion, we can be as politically correct as we want when filling government positions where lives aren't immediately at stake, but when public safety is at risk, we must have higher standards.

Beyond the loss of lives and the world's transformation after an event like 9/11, there's a profound sadness that lingers for a pilot like me. The innocence of a young boy in Nebraska, marveling at the wonders of aviation, dims in the face of evil that turns magic into dark sorcery. Those fateful terrorist attacks were not just an attack on our nation; they were an assault on the very essence of flight, a reminder of the darkness that can envelop even the most beautiful of human achievements. I look for silver linings in every hardship I've ever encountered. The silver lining I noticed after 9/11 was that we were united as a country, less easily offended over insignificant issues. Small things seemed to stay small, even if only for a small amount of time.

Pilots are a hard bunch to keep down. We land on our feet. We persist and endure. It's part of the job description. I hope to never again fly over a scene like the one I witnessed in 2001, but my determination and the spirit of flight keeps me rising from the ashes of tragedy.

10

Flying Closer to the Stars

In the late 1970s, when I was still flying the charter plane for Jim in Chadron, I experienced my first brush with celebrities. I flew a couple of Native Americans named Russell Means and Dennis Banks. The two men had made a name for themselves when they founded the American Indian Movement (AIM) in 1968, and further gained national recognition when they occupied Wounded Knee in 1973. Means, Banks, and about 200 Oglala Lakota Sioux activists seized control of Wounded Knee and forced a 71-day standoff with law enforcement and federal agents to draw attention to struggles faced by Native American communities. I remembered following this event on the news, since I'd been in high school at the time. More significantly, Wounded Knee is only about 60 miles from Chadron, so this was a news story that hit close to home. The men who'd previously been on my TV screen were now in the back of my plane.

Having now had numerous encounters with the rich and famous, I feel like it's reasonable to say that most of the tremendously rich or exceptionally famous people are also some of the nicest people. You have nothing they want, other than the ability to transport them from here to there. There's really no reason for them to be asses.

Bob and Dolores Hope became regular passengers.

An iconic and enduring figure of the entertainment industry, Bob Hope had traveled the world and was at home in a corporate plane. He loved to tell stories about other famous people. One of my favorite stories he told me was the time he and Frank Sinatra were in a parking lot in Las Vegas and Sinatra tipped the attendant $500. The attendant, while noticeably appreciative, was a bit taken back. He said, "Thank you, this is the biggest tip I've ever received." Sinatra responded, "What was the biggest tip you ever received before this?" "$100," the attendant replied. "And who gave you that?" Sinatra questioned. The attendant said, "You did, sir."

Before bottled water was mainstream, Dolores Hope once asked if there was any Perrier on board. Since we didn't have any available, I took advantage of a two-hour layover to run to a grocery store to purchase Perrier to serve on the airplane. As they were boarding the airplane, I proudly mentioned that Perrier water was now offered. Without missing a beat, Dolores asked, "Are the ice cubes made from Perrier water?"

Completely dumbfounded, I gaped at the air, trying to formulate an answer. Bob slapped me on the shoulder. "Of course, the ice cubes are made out of Perrier water," he said. "What kind of a pilot do you think we are dealing with?"

When Dolores wasn't looking, Bob looked at me and shrugged his shoulders, as if to say, *Follow my lead, son.*

Another time, the other pilots and I were staying in a hotel with adjoining suites. We had our door open, eating some grapefruit we had just bought in Phoenix. Bob Hope stuck his head in and said, "Boy, do those smell good. Can I have one?" He sat in our hotel room in his boxer shorts eating grapefruit with us. It's hard to be any more famous than Bob Hope, and yet he couldn't have been nicer.

I flew for a company where Johnny Carson was on the board of directors. We often flew guests in to be on *The Tonight Show*. Though the innovator of the late-night-talk-show format was charismatic on television, it was widely known that Carson was an introvert. A fellow aviation enthusiast, he owned his own airplane, almost identical to the one we were flying at the time. Carson would often pull away from the other passengers and spend his time bent over in the cockpit, talking to us. He seemed comfortable talking about aeronautical issues. I asked him once if he'd ever been to Chadron, Nebraska. He said his dad took him to the State Park once, which is a short drive south of town. He didn't say much after that. I assumed if he wanted us to know more, he would've said more.

Flying Johnny Carson around gave me an opportunity for even more celebrity run-ins. After a few times coming to a show, the show runners would start to recognize me and welcome me into the green room or allow me to wander around the halls before the start of a show. It's what I imagine reincarnation would feel like – seeing lots of people you feel you know, but none who know you. Once when I was entering through the gate of the Burbank Studios Entrance, someone called me by name, but they didn't immediately recognize Ron Howard, who was coming through security at the same time I was.

I was also in the studio audience the first night Ellen DeGeneres ever appeared on *The Tonight Show*. Johnny called her over to her desk and started her career. The other guest that night was Bob Hope, who we'd flown in earlier that evening.

If I was to give advice on how to conduct yourself around celebrities, it would be to treat them like family. Don't ask for favors, and don't act like you've never seen a celebrity before. Try to remember that they're just people like you. I may have broken a few of these rules when I had the honor to meet and fly Jimmy Doolittle, a true American hero and aviation pioneer. A legacy, both before and after his famous 'Doolittle Raid' during WWII, Doolittle left me a little starstruck. I have his autograph, which I asked for, and to this day, it is the only autograph I own. He instructed us to call him Jimmy, and he seemed to genuinely enjoy talking to people, especially pilots. If you didn't already know his long list of accolades and accomplishments, you'd never guess. He was that humble.

If Jimmy Doolittle was the most down to earth and kind celebrity I've ever met, Hillary Clinton was the most snakelike.

I worked for an airline that had a contract to fly Barack Obama and Hillary Clinton around during the campaign of 2008. It was common for airlines to do that, but not overly common that the same airline would fly opposing candidates. I flew both candidates several times, and it was an eye-opening experience to be on the campaign trail.

Our airline had a regulation that flight attendants were not allowed to open the airplane door if we were not in an approved jetway. The extremely heavy door could catch the wind and do thousands of dollars of damage to the airplane, so as a precaution, pilots were expected to handle this task. One day, I lost the coin flip, so it was my turn to open the door.

Hillary was seated in first class. She traveled with a make-up artist and hair stylist, who fixed her up before the door opened. As I opened the cockpit door, I could hear Hillary lambasting either her hair or makeup person. Hillary shouted names at her that would put this book in an entirely new rating category. She had an arrogant air of superiority around her that was just sickening.

We were trained to wait by the door until given instructions by the Secret Service to proceed. The small galley of the 737 felt even more compressed as I stood wait-ing for the nod from the Secret Service dude, while Hillary verbally ripped her employee to shreds. When at last the nod came, Hillary pasted a smile on her face, and out of the corner of her mouth she said to the Secret Service agent, "Now, stay the fuck out of my picture this time." He just nodded like he'd already heard this a million times, but if I were him, I wouldn't have taken a bullet for her.

Former President Bill Clinton had the total opposite effect on people. He was interesting, pleasant, unassum-ing. He oozed natural charisma. In his presence, people seemed to feel comfortable and at ease almost immedi-ately. If you needed an enjoyable type of guy to spend an afternoon drinking beer with, you'd pick someone like Bill Clinton. On the airplane, he would hand out hamburgers and beer to people like a flight attendant. Chelsea Clinton always seemed a little lost, perhaps just reserved, and it was evident that she was the most private of the Clinton family.

Former President Barack Obama, during the 2008 campaign, appeared to be a very nice gentleman. He al-ways made a point to talk to the pilots and to say things like, "Good morning, Don. How are things in Omaha?" I always assumed someone slipped him my name right be-fore he got on the plane. Once onboard, he would surround himself with people who would coach him on what to say and who to say it to. He had twice the secret service as Hil-lary, and it seemed like twice the handling. It felt a little unnerving to me as to how much his every action seemed controlled behind the scenes. Usually, when we arrived at a campaign stop, the pilots would watch the rally from the FBO. Obama would elegantly repeat what was just coached to him minutes before we'd landed. He must have had an incredible memory. Lots of reporters traveled with Obama. A CNN reporter once let us read the speech

Obama was going to give that evening. On paper it seemed very simple. To hear it on television that night, it was spoken with such elegance that I could see why so many people were convinced by it.

I flew Former President George H.W. Bush, Sr. before he was president, and Gerald Ford and Jimmy Carter after they were president. President Carter was the type of guy who could just as easily talk about nuclear engineering as he could discuss how much flux was needed to sweat a copper pipe. In fact, the former president appeared more intelligent in-person than he ever did on television. I flew Senator Bob Dole, who was kind and professional. Once he even invited me and another pilot to his family reunion in Kansas. Ben Carson, retired neurosurgeon and former politician, also flew with me. I appreciated his humble nature, which he demonstrated by spending time with the pilots and other staff members.

Secret Service agents are interesting people with haunting stories to tell, stories which seem almost unbelievable, except no one could make them up. The truth is way more unbelievable than fiction. As much as I'd like to drop names and be the big guy in the room, I'm pretty sure if I printed any of those stories, I'd be chased down, and my life would be jeopardized.

While Hillary Clinton was the most snakelike creature I'd ever flown, Marlin Perkins, Mutual of Omaha's *Wild Kingdom* host, placed an actual 180-pound snake on my shoulders. I stood in the cockpit, watching in fascination as the oversized prehistoric monster slithered towards me. Fortunately, Marlin had asked first if he could release it. Not sure whether this inspired the 2006 action thriller, Snakes on a Plane or not, but I'm afraid if I was caught unaware by a snake sliding into the cockpit, I'd probably try to stab it to death with my dinner fork. "Want to hold her?" Marlin asked.

I wasn't about to lose my cool in front of a TV host, and I must have made some sort of verbal commitment, because the next thing I knew the snake was being lifted onto my shoulders. At the time, I only weighed 175 pounds, and I had to square my knees beneath me. The snake was surprisingly tame. Marlin Perkins later retired from the show, and I also flew the new hosts, Jim Fowler and Peter Gross, along with countless monkeys, more snakes of all sizes, and other exotic animals.

Whitney Houston was by far the most beautiful human being I've ever seen. I flew her early in her career. When she arrived at the airport, her face was clear of makeup, her hair wild and loose. She wore casual clothes, no bra, and a tired smile. She seemed very nice, but distant, like she was probably tired of people staring at her. But it was hard not to.

Michael Jordan, basketball legend and global icon, was the tallest passenger I've ever flown. I flew him back to LA from Omaha. He slept the whole way.

Brooke Shields was one of the few actresses I met who was prettier in person than she was on screen. Tall and slender, her presence was a statement of grace.

I flew Frank Gifford, a former National Football League player and sports commentator, along with his wife, Kathie Lee Gifford, of *Live! With Regis and Kathie Lee*, and later *The Today Show*.

Nebraskans have a special love affair with college football, and Cornhusker football in particular, so my fellow Nebraskan readers will take special delight in hearing that I flew Tom Osborne, and even went on a fishing trip with him. He was a pleasant, nice, grandfatherly-type person. The other brush with Nebraska football fame was when I flew Danny Woodhead. He excelled at my alma mater, Chadron State College, and then went onto have a successful career in the NFL, including a Super Bowl appearance in 2012.

When it comes to the popcorn world, you can't get more famous than Orville Redenbacher. Orville and his grandson, Chip, were frequent passengers; and I often flew them into Omaha. It happened that they were in town for a big party at the same time my sister, Theresa, and her husband, Don Blausey, were visiting. I took them both to the party so they could meet the Popcorn King.

Robin Williams was the biggest A-List movie star I've ever flown. He was exactly how you would expect him to be. It was obvious he could make anyone laugh at any time for as long as he wanted.

I own a handmade guild guitar that's been with me for most of my life. When I had the chance to fly John Denver, I boarded it on the plane. To my surprise, John Denver played it for about an hour. I asked him to sign it for me, but he said, "No, I don't destroy good guitars." Had this happened in the days of the cell phone, I would have a picture of it. Years later, John Denver, who was also a fellow pilot, left on his last jet plane. Flying solo, his *Rutan Long-EZ*, a small, experimental single-engine plane he'd recently purchased, crashed. It's always a sad day to lose a comrade in the aeronautics world.

I've had many opportunities to meet and interact with the rich and famous during my time flying corporate planes. Other than being rich and famous, they are just people. I don't regret meeting most of them.

Those who are not in the airline industry will often refer to corporate flying as private, and airline flying as commercial. This is a pet peeve for me, because in aviation terminology, "commercial" specifically refers to the type of license a pilot has, meaning that with a commercial license, a pilot can be compensated for flying services. So whether or not a pilot is seated in the cockpit of a major airline or flying around at the beck and call of a movie star, if he's getting paid, he is technically a commercial pilot.

There are advantages and disadvantages to flying corporate. There were points in my career as a corporate pilot when I eyed the airlines with envy, hoping that the stars would realign so that I could be back in an airline job. Then, towards the end of my airline career, I was sure the corporate pilot job was the only one to have.

Today, as a semi-retirement gig, I'm back on the corporate side. I fly a beautiful *Dassault Falcon 50*, a three-engine jet, which belongs to a man who knows a little something about chasing dreams.

The first time I met Rick Collins was in the cockpit of a friend's Citation Jet. I was preparing for takeoff out of Pocatello, Idaho on a bitterly cold afternoon, when Rick strolled onto the plane. "Do you always wear that thing?" he asked, referring to my leather flying jacket.

"I always wear it 'til I'm sure we're going to clear the mountains," I replied.

Rick's laugh startled me. As distinctive as a comedy club filled with hyenas, I would soon be able to recognize that trademark guffaw within any 300-yard radius. Rick slapped his hand against my leather-clad shoulder. "I think we're going to get along just fine."

He was right. Rick hired me as his personal pilot in 2017. We soon became good friends.

Rick and I had more in common than the *Falcon 50*. Just like me, Rick knew from a young age what he wanted to do with his life. And at around 27 years-old, he became a millionaire doing just that.

Rick likes to say that most people sell cars because it's something they are forced into, or it was the only thing available at the time. But for Rick, it was what he always wanted to do, and if you do something you love, you'll never have to work a day in your life.

Rick Collins Toyota in Sioux City, Iowa is one of the biggest and best dealerships in the area. It was built from the ground up, with a lot of hard work and a little bit of luck. Part of Rick's luck came about when he married Pam, who is not only one of the nicest people I've ever met, but also an early proponent of this book.

Whenever Rick's around a group of people, I like to tell them, "If it wasn't for me, Rick wouldn't be where he is today." It always gets a laugh.

Flying for the Collinses has probably been one of the most enjoyable jobs I've ever had. They keep me in warm climates during the winter, and in cool mountain air during the summer.

Of course, not all corporate jobs are so wonderful. Some corporations I've flown for include Mutual of Omaha, ConAgra, Bridal Fair, Henningson, Durham, and Richardson (HDR) Inc., and Circo Enterprises. I've provided pilot services for banks, oil companies, investment firms, trucking companies, law firms, an irrigation company, a business that builds commercial shelving, and even a company that makes the sterile cotton balls that you find in the empty space of your Aspirin bottle.

One big difference between corporate and airline flying is the personal level at which a corporate pilot can get to know passengers. As a corporate pilot, I've become an intricate part of a company, directly interacting with the CEO or top-level company officials on a regular basis. Instead of saying 'thank you' and 'have a nice day' to 150 commercial passengers as they file past the main cabin door, I've had opportunities to have long conversations with corporate passengers over dinners and other events. In addition to fewer passengers, corporate flying jobs also have smaller crews, which can also foster closer friendships.

There's a higher potential for pay in an airline job, though neither offers a steady income. Schedules are rigid for commercial pilots; whereas, corporate pilots are at the mercy of a company's specific needs and sporadic travel schedules. A corporate pilot's layover can be anywhere from one and a half hours to 20 days. Long layovers were torture when I was a young pilot. I just wanted to get home and spend time with my family. Now that I'm an old pilot, the long layovers are wonderful. With fewer responsibilities at home, I can enjoy the time we spend at various destinations, whether it's relaxing at the beach, or exploring a mountain resort.

Whether piloting an airline or corporate plane, the flying part is generally the same. You go up, you go down, and you are responsible for more people's lives in those few hours than a surgeon will see in his entire career.

Ground operation responsibilities are vastly different.

Most commercial airlines I've worked for require you to be in the cockpit approximately 15 minutes before pushback. Perfecting pre-flight protocol is essential for every pilot. An important component of this procedure is to look cool while doing it. Safety, while obviously the first concern, can only be enhanced by a crisply ironed uniform and a well-practiced saunter when approaching the boarding gate. Here, the gate agent hands you a huge stack of important-looking paperwork that someone else prepared for you, further boosting your level of coolness. Aviator sunglasses also help. Next, you check fuel loads, and hopefully you've already checked weather conditions. Several signatures are required. Then you head inside to go through your pre-flight checklist.

Obviously this is a simplification, but in an airline, the pilot is working with a whole crew of people who are responsible for everything that happens to the plane both before you ever get on board and after you leave the airport at the end of your flight. The airline even has a scheduling department that handles things like hotels, ground transportation, meals, adequate duty, rest, and current legal documents.

Alternatively, a corporate pilot often assumes most of the responsibility with airplane maintenance and the pre-flight planning and preparation–which sometimes takes days, weeks, or even months before takeoff. Everything in that fat pack of important documents that was handed to the airline pilot is necessary for the corporate pilot to obtain and study. Upon landing, the pilot's job is only beginning. The plane must be properly stowed for the time that it might sit outside, or moved into a hangar if one is available. In winter months, you need to check if deicing will be available. This is also the time to track down any needed tools required for ground operations, such as towbars, ground power units, catering, and cleaning supplies. The passengers, as well as the plane, need a place to stay, and booking hotel rooms is another task often handled by the corporate pilot. Ground transportation, directions to restaurants, and various reservations are also frequently on the pilot's task list. In my current position, it's often my responsibility to go get Rick's Porsche and make sure it's running. As an extra act of goodwill, I feel that it is my responsibility to ensure that it still accelerates very quickly.

A challenging aspect of being a corporate pilot is that nothing is ever the same. That's also the most enjoyable part.

Whether flying for an airline or a corporate operation, pilots transport people. But what if a person wants to make a living as a pilot, but doesn't want to constantly be around passengers? It's no easy task dealing with constant complaints, making accommodations for varying needs, and trying to make ice cubes out of Perrier. But a third option does exist; and that's the story of the freight pilot.

11

The Other Side of the Clock

The first officer adjusted the pressurization system. I felt the plane shift as we began our descent into darkness. The obsidian sky was layered in clouds, obliterating the view for any would-be stargazers. Instead, the stars were scattered on the ground below us, the sleeping city twinkling in the dead of night. A lot of people think that landing a plane at night is like trying to hit a Christmas tree. But the runway at night is more like swaths of ink spills compared to the glowing city. Runway lights form constellations that lead us to the landing lanes, which from the sky look just like dark empty fingers pointing us towards the airport.

More than anything, I wanted to land and go to bed.

Over the radio, I heard an inexperienced pilot having a hard time locating the airport. Finding an airport at night is always a challenge no matter how experienced a pilot is; though after seeing a thousand airports from the sky, it becomes easier. It was evident the air controller was growing frustrated with the new pilot. "It's the big bright spot with all the lights. You can't miss it."

"That's certainly not going to help the pilot," I told the first officer. "The airport looks more like a big dark spot."

He agreed and we continued the descent. The first officer and I had been flying night freight for a few months now, so we could almost make this route in our sleep; and believe me, we were tempted. Flying at night can be challenging, simply because it's harder to see in the black air. I once read about a pilot flying over the Great Plains on a starlit night. The lights on the ground were sparse, but they were ample in the sky. He wrote how he confused the sky with the ground. Lights can appear to be much closer than they are, and weather makes distances even more difficult to judge.

But fortunately on this night, the runways were dry and the wind was still. Our wheels thumped against the pavement, and the tires squealed in momentary protest as they battled with friction on the initial contact. The sun was about to rise, and I wanted nothing more than a mattress and eight hours. As we taxied toward the terminal, I began my mental checklist of all the things I'd need to do before I could finally sleep. Paperwork, overseeing cargo handling, security checks, post-flight inspection, maintenance notifications ... none of it sounded as appealing as a comforter pulled over my head.

The year I spent flying nighttime freight took years off my life.

My body fought a constant battle as to whether it should be asleep or awake. I've been fortunate not to succumb to bouts of depression, but nighttime freight brought me right to the edge.

This is probably the reason why I have so many clear memories of flying airlines and corporate planes throughout my career, but my memories of freight flying are more like the dream you try to grasp upon waking, but the harder you reach, the fuzzier the dream becomes. I know people who thrive on this schedule, but I'm too fond of sleeping when it's dark and being awake when it's light rather than ending my nights watching the sunrise.

The pilots who fly on the other side of the clock call themselves freight dogs. The pilots who fly the smaller feeder planes into the main hubs at night call themselves feeder dogs. I'm not sure where the terminology comes from because the dogs I've known tend to sleep all the time. But if you ever get a chance to talk with a freight dog or feeder dog, the main topic of conversation will likely be about sleep. Other pilots talk about women and families and rock 'n' roll. All a freight pilot talks about is how much sleep he got yesterday and how much he hopes to get today.

Most airports take on an entirely different personality at night. Parts of the aerodrome are so dark and quiet that it's hard to imagine it will ever come back to life. Instead of passengers crammed into every nook and cranny, there might be one janitor slowly maneuvering an industrial sized floor scrubber down the echoing terminals.

A few airports in the country get even busier at night. Places like Louisville, Kentucky; Memphis, Tennessee; and Dayton, Ohio are known for their nighttime freight hubs. On the darkest of nights, these airports are lit up like daytime, and can become some of the busiest air traffic control areas in the country.

While the rest of the country sleeps, the nighttime freight business operates effectively and efficiently. The post office moves a tremendous amount of their freight through these overnight operations. The whole procedure is so slick that it's almost easier to get a letter across the country than it is to get it across town. FedEx, UPS, and other delivery services own fleets of airplanes to move goods across the country. Everything is flown by freight flyers—from electronics, textiles, and produce to aquatic animals, livestock, and heavy machinery. Nothing smells like a plane filled with white lab rats. Flying through the dark, the smell wafts into the cockpit with such intensity that at times I could almost feel them crawling up my legs. I'll tell you that a baby elephant is also an odorous flight companion; and special preparation of the aircraft is needed to protect against the corrosiveness of elephant urine. Planeloads of broccoli don't smell half as bad in comparison.

A real benefit to freight flying is that freight doesn't complain about delays. Of course, the people waiting for the freight are a different story.

During my year as a freight dog, the most interesting cargo I ever flew was human organs. I had a short stint with a company that flew demand charter, and part of that business plan included organ retrieval. Though I've been an organ donor since I checked the box on my first driver's license, I never imagined such an elaborate system in place to obtain the organs.

Human organ transportation by air began in the 1960s, and with technological advancement both in the medical field and aviation, patients in-need of organ donations no longer required proximity to donors for successful transplantation. The ability to match donors with patients across the country and to transport organs quickly opened new opportunities for life-saving surgeries.

Organs have tight time limits in order to keep them useful. The ischemic time, or the amount of time an organ can survive without blood flow, varies depending on the organ. If you have flown on a lot of commercial flights, chances are you've shared a plane with a human kidney. Thousands of human organs fly on commercial flights each year. Each day, as many as ten organs are flying across the country on passenger planes. The majority of these are kidneys since they can remain viable outside of the body for up to 36 hours.

The next time you complain about lost luggage after a flight, just be glad someone didn't lose your liver. Unfortunately, human error, weather delays, and other nuisances which affect travelers, can also have severe consequences for human organs. According to the United Network for Organ Sharing, seven percent of human organs are lost, damaged, or encounter transportation troubles that render them unusable.

The heart and lungs can only be preserved for up to six hours, making quick transportation essential. These more time-sensitive organs rely on private jets, helicopters, and charter planes, like the ones I flew.

The process started with a phone call; then a team of doctors and nurses would arrive at the airplane by ambulance, personal car, or even helicopter, whichever option was the fastest. Depending on the donor and viable organs, several jets and surgical teams might arrive at the airport in order to transport body parts to different patients all over the country. It would take a poet to adequately describe the surgical teams arriving at the airport carrying small coolers, loading onto the planes, and departing in separate directions. During those moments, I imagined the donor's spirit floating above the scene, watching his organs depart east, west, north, and south, flying off in individual jets to save the lives of many other people. Someone who had so recently been whole was experiencing the ultimate diaspora.

From the pilot seat, I couldn't help but feel part of this phenomenal team, knowing that my job was truly about to change the life of someone. As the medical professionals hastened towards the waiting planes, I thought about the individual who donated the organs, and the loss to that person's family. I thought about the patients who were waiting for these organs, and the hope that this precious cargo would bring. The science, skill, and circumstances of the whole process was more than I could wrap my mind around.

Organ transport units are often given priority airspace, facilitating rapid takeoffs and landings; but despite the hurried nature of our ventures, I often had opportunities to talk with the transport team. Surprisingly, plenty of light moments between the pilots and medical staff occurred. The airplanes usually provided catered food to help fuel the long night ahead; and I can't tell you how many jokes I heard about which cooler had the food in it. The jokes keep your mind going from somewhere it probably shouldn't. One nurse opened her catering box and said, "Why is it always rare beef and spaghetti?"

A sense of humor goes a long way to ease traumatic situations. Rookie first-responders are especially prone to becoming emotional on the job. One person told me, "When you stop to think about it, the rookie is the only one with a normal response to such a scene. We are the sick ones used to such trauma." I think the dark humor is a coping mechanism to help these workers keep a clear head in the midst of carnage.

A person doesn't soon forget flying a human organ from one part of the country to another. I frequently think about the people who might be walking around today, still alive thanks to an organ I delivered.

At the end of a freight flying shift, I was never able to go home and sleep. With the mid-morning sun shining brightly overhead, my brain would battle against my body and keep me wired. When the afternoon rolled around and I smacked hard against the wall of exhaustion, I figured at that point, I might as well just stay awake until dark. When the sun sank low on the Nebraska plains, at last, I slipped into sleep. The next morning, my body would feel normal.

But my mind knew that somewhere, it had missed a day.

12

Mile-High Comedy Club

The clock ticked down to our scheduled departure time. We sat at the gate in Dallas, Texas, and I anxiously keyed the intercom. "What's the story? Can we expedite this boarding process?"

I could hear the sigh in the flight attendant's answer. "We're doing the best we can. Seems like no one's in a hurry."

It's a coordinated crew effort to load a plane of passengers. Aisles must be cleared so that people can squeeze past with their luggage and stuff bags into overhead compartments. Everyone must be seated and buckled. There's always at least one passenger who requests a change of seat at the last minute, which can feel like a game of Tetris. This was my cue to use my PA privileges. "Alrighty folks, every single one of my exes lives in this state. I would certainly appreciate it if you could hurry things along. I would like to leave as soon as possible."

According to the flight attendants, several passengers immediately broke into the chorus of, "All my exes live in Texas." What could have been a stressful situation and a delayed flight, became a sing-along with cooperative customers and an on-time departure.

You can divide the world in half with a microphone. Bring one out, and half the population would say,

"My God, get that thing away from me."

The other half says, "Oh great, a microphone. Let me have it."

I fall squarely into the second group. I've always fancied myself as a wannabe stand-up comedian; but as a pilot, I'm forced to sit during my job. I've always had a captive audience, because once the doors are pressurized on an aircraft, there's no opening them.

Take a plane full of trapped passengers, a microphone at my disposal, and the perk that the audience will only glimpse the back of my head, and you've created a monster.

Comedians and pilots have more in common than you might realize. Both provide escape. Comedians allow audiences to escape into a world of laughter; and pilots grant escape by whisking the passengers away to new destinations. I've always admired great comedians, finding solace in their wit and humor. George Carlin with his sharp insight, and Dave Chappelle with his uncanny ability to connect to an audience, have become my sources of inspiration.

Imagine that instead of being world class comedians, George Carlin and Dave Chappelle were two of my crewmembers. Of course, we'd have to assume these two didn't indulge in their usual vices on the job. Cigarettes and weed are not allowed in the cockpit, only raw talent.

If George Carlin were the pilot, his passengers might be nervously intrigued, caught between the discomfort of government critique and the assurance of existential acceptance. In the realm of Dave Chappelle's flight, diversity would thrive, breaking down barriers and fostering laughter across all divides. In this fanciful scenario, each passenger regardless of his seat—would be enveloped in an atmosphere of warmth and humor.

It's obvious that comedians pay incredible attention

to detail. They dissect everyday life and mundane situations and turn them into comedy. Pilots, too, must be detail-oriented, managing complicated maneuvers, communications with the control tower, and keeping alert for unexpected situations. A comedian's ability to swiftly address hecklers could easily translate into managing emergencies in an airplane.

Weather delays, technical difficulties, connections that can't be missed all make traveling stressful—add the thought of visiting relatives at the end of your flight, and you might start to question why people travel at all. If there's no joy in the journey, what's the point? So I do my best to bring the fun wherever I go.

What's more fun than the PA system on an airplane? To be honest, I could probably name a few things, but when you are on an airplane, the PA system ranks highly. "Sit back and relax and enjoy the flight. If you'd like, however, it's your option to lean forward and be tense."

I'd like to think I could fly with the same crew for 30 days and not repeat any of my material. It's my estimation that the passengers in the back don't hear 90 percent of what comes from the cockpit anyway, nor do they likely care which direction we are flying or at what altitude. Most passengers probably side with Jerry Seinfeld when he said something like, "Just try to land at the place that is printed on the ticket."

Sometimes I play games for my own amusement. "It's time to push back," I say. "I need all passengers over 6 feet tall to duck down so I can see behind me to back this thing out." There's always a few who fall for it, followed by the sound of laughter as the joke hits its mark.

To break up the monotony on a long flight, it's fun to say, "Ladies and gentlemen, in my 40 years of flying, I've only seen this a couple of times, if you want to look out your right window..." I then count to three. "Oh, sorry, now it's on your left side." The entire passenger group swings from one side to the other in a synchronized movement. I remember a flight attendant calling up to the cockpit telling me how funny it looked and that I should do it again. I explained to him the joke only works one time per flight.

Holidays provide extra opportunities to connect with passengers over the PA system. I love doing Santa sightings at altitude for the young and young-at-heart during Christmastime. I remember one young girl approached me after the flight, her facial expression filled with absolute glee. "I saw him! I really saw Santa!"

Once on July 4, departing out of St. Louis for a short hop to Chicago, I wished all the passengers a Happy Fourth of July, adding, "If there are any British passengers on board, get over it, you lost." As luck would have it, a person with a strong British accent asked me upon deplaning if there were guidelines as to what I could and could not say on the PA system. In my best British accent, I said, "Nope. We did away with those right after the war."

I've only been written up a few times in my career for my PA communications, and usually this has come from another employee who was somehow offended. Being offended is a big deal today. If I haven't offended you, it's just because you haven't stuck around long enough. Readers of this book can close it if they get offended; but at 30,000 feet in the air, none of my passengers has that luxury.

Not everyone finds me funny. During a flight, I announced, "If any passengers today carried kryptonite on board, please secure it in lead containers and do not open it during flight. It affects me severely up here and could be detrimental to the safety of the flight should you choose to open the container."

As you might've guessed, a few weeks later the

company got a letter explaining how a passenger did not think the joke was funny and that it did not add to the enjoyment of his flight.

A joke I told for 20 years was, "Welcome aboard ladies and gentlemen. You have three of the finest flight attendants on board today and one regular one." On this particular flight, I hadn't had much of a chance to meet the flight attendants before takeoff, and of course one of them took offense, no doubt the one assuming the identity of the 'regular one.' A note was written to the company, and when my boss contacted me, I said, "For God's sake Bob, I've used that joke for 20 years."

It's funny that it was Bob Stienke who received the complaint, as he and I had a long history of flying together. We'd sometimes do the "Bob and Don" show for passengers. I'd start out by saying something like, "Good morning ladies and gentlemen, welcome to the Bob and Don show. Hello Bob." Bob would of course respond, "Hello Don." Bob could do so many different voices, each more exaggerated and ridiculous than the next, and he'd stay in character for the whole leg of that flight. One time a passenger actually asked, "Where are the real pilots?"

Bob was a hoot, even though I came close to wetting my pants a few times.

Sometimes my PA announcements came in the form of inside jokes with other crew members. I didn't know much about it at the time, but it turns out that South America is a great place to do Brazilian waxes. If you are into that type of thing, it's something you should plan on scheduling the next time you are south of the border. The reason I know about Brazilian waxes is because we had a long van ride between our hotel and the airport during one of our international flights. I was traveling with three female flight attendants, one male flight attendant, a first-crew officer, and a mechanic. The driver did not speak

English. Two of the female flight attendants openly discussed their Brazilian wax experiences. They spoke with stereotypically loud American voices; so despite the private nature of their conversation, the conversation was categorically not private. Apparently, they'd given euphemistic names to the body parts which had just been waxed. One flight attendant said at full volume, "My Chuckie is so sore, I don't think I'll be recovering from this for at least a few days." The other flight attendant answered at an equally raucous volume. "Really? My Glenda feels a lot better than I expected it would."

Once we were in the airplane and getting ready to push back, I always liked to introduce the flight attendants to the passengers, especially if I knew them personally. "Good morning, ladies and gentlemen. Welcome aboard today. You are lucky to have four of the finest flight attendants in the company on-board today. In the back, we have Cindy and John. Serving you up front will be Chuckie and Glenda."

Of course, the passengers had no idea what we were talking about, but the crew and I still laugh about it today.

I once used the PA system to draw some unwanted attention to a friend. Raymo, as everyone called him, had just completed a long day and fortuitously snagged an empty seat in the back of one of my flights. I tried, but could not resist my love-affair with the microphone. "Ladies and gentlemen, now that you've settled in, I have a quick announcement to make. We have a very distinguished passenger on board. I'm proud to introduce Mike Raymond. A former 747 pilot and NASA astronaut, he has recently become a Vision Airline pilot. Raymo has spent more time in the space shuttle than any other human being. At his young age, his aviation accomplishments are phenomenal. I know he would be very happy to answer any questions you might have about aviation or NASA.

Welcome aboard, Captain Raymo."

To my delight, I later found out that the flight was packed with children, all wanting to meet this 'famous astronaut.' Raymo signed autographs and kept kids entertained throughout the entire flight. I'm sure he wanted to strangle me, but he didn't have the heart to disappoint the young children. I wonder how many children still treasure his autograph, or are now themselves astronauts at NASA because they were inspired by Raymo. Hopefully they never went looking for his name in the employee records.

The term 'low-cost airlines' has always been an amusing concept to me, given the unbelievable costs associated with flight. I'm never quite sure if the passengers understand the irony. During some delays, flight attendants are not allowed to get up, because we may begin taxiing at any moment. I use this time to inform the passengers about the brand-new airplane they've boarded. "This shiny new airplane cost about $40 million. Each engine is worth around $5 million. It costs in the neighborhood of $10,000 an hour to keep this thing in the air. Lift and drag are only emergency backup procedures in case the company runs out of money while we are airborne. Now sit back and relax on this low-cost airline."

If you've had any experience in airports, you know that planes do not always leave or arrive on time. Some passengers take this as a personal attack. One of my announcements during a delay would be, "I know we're delayed. We're doing everything we can to move it along. Please, rest-assured I will not jeopardize your safety for your comfort." That comment usually took a few minutes to sink in.

Understanding the challenges of travel, particularly for solo parents, has made me more attuned to the little ways I can make a difference. When I see a young mother wrestling luggage with three children by herself, I offer to help. I was always amazed at how quickly she would hand me a kid and continue to struggle with her unwieldy suitcase. It must be the uniform. It was fun to ask the kids questions like, "Hey, do you know what you need? You need a puppy!" Most of the time it would make the mother smile and the kids laugh.

At the end of a flight, the pilot always says something to the effect of, "Thank you for flying with us today. If this is your final destination, we hope you enjoy your stay." I imagine George Carlin would listen to those words but hear something different. "Aviation is just a million moving parts around an oil leak, so tighten those seatbelts, folks, because this jumble of parts is pointed to the ground at 600 miles per hour."

Mark Twain once said, "The human race has only one really effective weapon, and that is laughter."

These days, there's a trend of taking everything so seriously, even aviation. But being too serious is a drag. And part of a pilot's job is to reduce drag since it can affect the performance of an airplane. As long as you aren't too offended, laughter can go a long way in bringing people together. The similarities between the comedic world and the piloting world remind me that in the scheme of life, we're all just crewmembers finding our way through this cosmic journey. If we can laugh our way through that journey, all the better.

13

Delayed

When a flight is delayed, passenger maturity levels plummet. Common sense and reasoning disappear. Take an extremely intelligent individual, put them in an airport, add a delay, and somehow that person loses all brain capacity. This is obviously a broad generalization; and I know that you, reader, have never overreacted to a flight delay, but you'd be surprised at some of the things I've seen over my career.

Here are a few PA announcements that I've been tempted to make from the cockpit, but fortunately my last shreds of self-control kept me from grabbing the microphone.

Okay, screaming, rude passengers. Sit down and put your seatbelts on. Keep your feet off the seat in front of you, and I'll take this broken airplane into the sky. If the only way to make you happy is to risk scattering your body parts across the field, I'm just about tempted to get this plane moving. Or *Good afternoon, passengers. The weather is so bad that the birds are walking. But we will go ahead and fly if it will shut you up.* Or *To the loudly complaining, uneducated passenger in the back, guess what? Pilots hate delays too. We have places to go, events to attend, and lives to live. Believe it or not, I am not delaying this flight just to see you in pain.*

Once at Dallas International, I was waiting at a gate to see if my jump seat was going to come through. The flight had been delayed, and an elderly man in front of me was taking out his frustrations on the gate agent. As he became more agitated, his cane lifted from the ground, and just as he began swinging it across the desk towards the gate agent, I grabbed it and confiscated it from him. It was by no means a Kung Fu move. He was old and slow. I probably could've caught the cane in my teeth without dental damage, but attempting to whack a gate agent with a cane is not okay. He was old enough to know better.

"What the hell is wrong with you?" I demanded.

He began to explain his situation.

I interrupted him. "Oh, excuse me, you misunderstood my question. I don't care."

I handed his cane to the gate agent. "Here, you can do with this what you want."

"A lot of the passengers are getting testy," the agent said, taking the cane from my hand.

It had been a long wait. We were waiting for the jetway driver to enter the gate and offload the passengers, but because the gates were controlled by the city, there wasn't anything we could do about it on our end. I took the mic and made an announcement. "This gate is controlled by the city. This isn't an issue with the airline."

That didn't help.

I went back to the microphone. "If anyone here has the mayor's personal phone number, I would be glad to call her."

It just so happened that one of our passengers had high connections. Someone handed me the number. I dialed it, and it appeared to be a legitimate number. I grabbed the mic again and announced the number to all the passengers, suggesting they all call her immediately.

Miracle of miracles, someone was there to open the gate shortly.

The old adage in the service industry is that the customer is always right. But let's be honest, most passengers do not have extensive aeronautical knowledge; therefore, they can't always be right because they don't really know what's going on. Passenger safety must trump passenger desire. Yet, all you have to do is turn on the news for a few minutes to see the latest stories of passengers throwing tantrums because they did not get their way. Back in 2013, a passenger made headlines after being told he couldn't use the restroom while the plane was preparing for takeoff. He became so unruly that he announced he'd hidden explosives in his toothpaste. The plane had to be evacuated and the passenger was arrested. I wonder how long he had to wait to use the bathroom after he was put in handcuffs.

Years ago, one of my flights was delayed because a guy beat up his girlfriend on the jetway. We had to suspend our takeoff to give paramedics a chance to get in there and do their job. As I was already in the cockpit, I didn't witness this event firsthand, but I've always wondered why other people didn't step in to help, or if they just stepped over the poor girl to board the plane.

Alcohol is routinely the root cause of unruly passengers. I've often told my flight attendants, "If you don't want them on board, I don't want them on board." Back before 9/11, captains would sometimes send a copilot into the cabin to assist flight attendants in wayward situations. During one particular flight, a flight attendant buzzed through with a complaint. "Hey, we've got a rowdy back here," she said.

The captain looked at me. "Go see what you need to

do."

I unbuckled and could hear the yelling as soon as I opened the cabin door. "If you don't shut that kid up, I'm going to shut him up for you!" I saw a twenty-something year-old man standing menacingly over a woman with a screaming toddler. The flight attendant was trying to stand between them, but she was no match for the man's bulky size.

"Hey, back off," I shouted, hurtling myself down the aisle. "Just what the hell do you think you're doing?"

The man turned to look at me and staggered sideways with the effort. I could tell he was wasted even before I smelled the pungent scent of alcohol. "This lady won't shut her kid up," he slurred.

"Look here," I said. "You are going to sit down, fasten your seat belt, and stare at the seatback tray in front you. If you so much as glance away from that tray, I'm going to land this plane and have you arrested."

He remained seated through the rest of the flight. The flight attendant kept calling on the intercom to give us progress reports. "He hasn't looked away once," she quipped. "He's just staring straight ahead."

When the plane landed, the cops were there at the end of the jetway ready to handcuff the guy. "This is bullshit," his furious gaze fixed on me. "You said if I sat down and stared at that thing, you wouldn't have me arrested."

"Well," I said. "I lied. Enjoy prison."

Today when a passenger gets out of hand, pilots aren't allowed to leave the cockpit. My management skills often consist of, "Call security, have them arrested, and lock my door." Throughout my career, I would guess I've had close to 20 people removed from my plane, and at least 19 of those involved alcohol.

Another time, before pushback, a flight attendant told me that an elderly woman in the back was irate and refused to buckle her seatbelt. Since we hadn't engaged the plane yet, I went back to see if I could smooth things over.

"What seems to be the problem?"

"I was supposed to have priority boarding," she spit out the words. "Elderly people are supposed to preboard, but they didn't let me."

"Ma'am, I'm sorry to hear that. I have an open seat in first class, and I'm happy to move you up there to make up for this mistake."

"This is outrageous," she spewed. "This is unacceptable. The gate agent stood right out there and said I wasn't allowed to preboard!"

"I can see you are really upset," I said. "It looks like we have a couple of choices here. I can get on the mic and have everyone deplane right now, and then we can board again and make sure that you can get on first, if that's what it's going to take to make you happy."

"That seems stupid."

"I'd have to agree, that does seem pretty stupid. The other option is that you can move up to that empty seat in first class, and you can order yourself some drinks. The booze will be on me."

When we landed at our destination, the crew had to order a wheelchair for the old lady, because she was too drunk to walk out of the plane on her own power. It must have been a sight, watching a white-haired granny prototype pound miniature bottles of rum. On the bright side, we didn't hear any more complaints about preboarding.

To be fair, I've flown far more polite people than problematic passengers. I've often said you spend 90-percent of your time dealing with 10-percent of people. Unfortunately, it's that 10-percent I remember most vividly. I have tremendous respect for gate agents and flight attendants on the frontlines of all the passenger interactions.

If there is anything that I'm an undisputed expert on, it's waiting.

As a personal mental exercise, I used to calculate how much money I would make if I was forced to enter a holding pattern, was delayed on the ground, or had to return to the gate for a mechanical issue. The old *Boeing 727* had a flight clock, which was the method the company used to calculate our monthly paycheck. It consisted of a simple switch on the door, probably not unlike the switch in your refrigerator that turns the light on. Common practice was to enlist a flight attendant to hold that switch for a few seconds while we released the parking brake, reset it, and then we'd be on the clock getting paid.

Whether the pilot is on or off the clock, the grander clock of life keeps ticking. With so much time waiting, it becomes important how a pilot uses those in-between hours. For a good part of my career I prioritized exercising, increasing my knowledge through reading and watching documentaries, visiting local libraries, and exploring new places. These last few years, I've carried around my airplane guitar, which is a full-sized acoustic that looks like something Willie Nelson would own. I used to carry a small travel-type guitar, but it just looked silly at open-mics in strange towns.

Hopefully all this sounds impressive, but you should know that I've also watched more episodes of *Gunsmoke*, *Andy Griffith*, *Family Guy*, and *South Park* than I could even begin to calculate.

Many common practices in the travel world just add to the waiting time. Most hotel check-out times are set at 11 a.m., but a normal departure time in my job is 4 p.m. These days, I've become accustomed to waiting, and can fill my time with a late breakfast and a late lunch. I've expanded my pallet and my waistline by searching for new restaurants on the road. When a new flight plan gets announced, I immediately think of my favorite restaurant and favorite menu items in the area. It's hard not to indulge, but local cuisine and an expense account make choosing a healthy lifestyle a secondary option.

I wasn't always an old pilot and I'm sympathetic to the stress of waiting, unexpected delays while traveling, and even to the frustrating feeling of not having control over your situation. My adult son, Rob, and I were driving through Colorado not too long ago. I told him a story about his sixth birthday party, and how I'd been stuck in Colorado Springs with a mechanical delay. All I wanted was to get home for my son's birthday. The delay stretched out long enough that I was released because I'd timed out, so I rented a car to get to Denver International Airport. I contributed to the chaos of the maddening rush-hour commute, weaving in and out of traffic, and acting just like the idiots that I usually cussed at, all to make a flight that would get me to Omaha in time for the party. I reached the gate just in time, secured my seat, and walked into the party with just moments to spare—the stress all worth it to see my son's face light up with the glow of his six candles.

After sharing this story, Rob said, "I don't even remember my sixth birthday party."

There are countless reasons that airplanes are delayed. Weather and mechanical issues top the list. It's astonishing how many customers complain during the deicing process. As an experienced pilot, I know that airplanes don't fly with ice on them. Ice changes the shape of the airfoil, and the shape of the airfoil is how the airplane produces lift to stay in the sky. Years ago, a flight attendant told me that a little girl didn't think her side of the plane was deiced. We had a good chuckle over this, but since we were in communication with the deicing crew, I asked them if they'd deiced the left wing yet. He said, "No, but we're getting there." I was impressed with that young kid. If she'd been several years older, I would have bought her a drink.

I will always remember a time when the TSA delayed our flight because they changed their mind on whether a woman should be allowed to carry the ashes of her deceased husband on board. The widow, who hadn't been told of this decision, was already aboard the airplane. A TSA agent entered the plane and was asking her to relinquish the ashes. There was no way I was going to let this happen, so I stepped in, explaining to the agent that the ashes weren't going anywhere. I asked the woman if she'd be okay with me explaining the situation to her fellow passengers. "Go ahead," she said. "This is the most ridiculous thing I've ever heard of."

Instead of hiding in the flight deck, I came out and faced the passengers. Standing in front of them in the galley I made my announcement over the PA system. "This delay is entirely on my shoulders, and it is my responsibility. We have a passenger who would like to carry her husband's ashes on the flight, and this TSA agent is not allowing it. I'm not moving this plane until I can get authority to have this agent removed." I delayed that flight for one hour and ten minutes until I had authority to remove the agent. After the flight, as the passengers were deplaning, I made sure to stand at the front so I could take the brunt of the complaints, rather than the flight attendants. To my surprise, a good number of passengers were polite and thanked me for helping. Several told me that it was the right thing to do.

That is the only time I have ever delayed an airplane for personal reasons.

Here's a story I can tell you, but only because the

airline involved went out of business, and I don't really care what the Feds have to say. Once a woman's dog caused a slight delay. The pup's carrier wouldn't fit in the seat in front of her. I've always said that I like most dogs better than I like most humans, so we let the dog sit up front with us on the jump seat. I even took a picture of the dog wearing my hat and my ID clipped to his collar. I stopped short of getting up and putting him in the left seat and having him put his paws on the control yoke, though it did cross my mind.

It should be no surprise that the award for the strangest delay ever involves an airplane toilet. When toilets flush on an airplane, there is a tremendous amount of suction produced. Shortly before it was time to close the doors and push back, one of our flight attendants, Mary, came to the cockpit. "I have a passenger stuck on the toilet in the back."

This didn't seem to be an issue. "Tell her to finish up and get to her seat," I said.

"No," Mary hesitated. "It's different. It seems she is not able to get off the seat."

Apparently, this passenger's rear end was the perfect mathematical equivalent to create a seal when the toilet flushed, the suction fastening her securely to the toilet seat. The paramedics were called, and to this day I still have questions. First, why was she still seated when she flushed the toilet? Second, what tool did they use to relieve the pressure and get her off the toilet seat? Third, how did Mary handle herself with such professional grace? She allowed the passenger to have all the dignity that was humanly possible in such an awkward situation. I don't think I'd have had the whereabouts or the maturity to handle the situation as well as she did.

No one likes a flight delay, least of all a pilot. But being a pilot extends beyond the flightdeck. In the midst of chaos and anxiety of unexpected waiting, pilots have an opportunity to extend patience and understanding to passengers. Embracing the unpredictable nature of my job, I know that each delay and each unruly passenger is a chance to demonstrate resilience and grace under pressure.

14

From Coffee Pots to Cockpits: SOPs for Every Occasion

In addition to a lifetime of studying aeronautics, I think I could also count myself as somewhat of an expert in the field of philosophy. When you're flying over oceans and mountain ranges, you've got a lot of time to think. During my many hours up in the sky, I've had the luxury to ponder various concepts and ideas; and I've come to the realization that a pilot's approach to life can be adapted for almost all of life's situations.

In the rarefied air of a pilot's ruminations, where oxygen is sparse and thoughts soar to higher levels, this chapter contains my profound insights. Take this book, find a comfy spot on your couch, and enjoy the wisdom of a philosophy that I've come to call *A Pilot's Guide to Successful Living*.

Pilots have been described in many ways and not all of them are complimentary. I've heard arrogant, narcissistic, and cocky. This outward appearance of egotism has less to do with a pilot's prideful attitude, and more to do with a finely tuned internal mechanism that makes us believe we are right; after all, lives depend on it. This self-assuredness comes from extensive training, thorough planning, checklists, backup plans for every emergency, and backup plans for backup plans.

Pilots are trained to be consistent in their planning, which begins as soon as they are notified of a trip. Everything is on a checklist, and the list is checked twice. There is a system for every situation, a methodical blueprint for each setting and circumstance. Just about every disturbance can be avoided by checking and double checking all the information available to a pilot before a flight.

Imagine if we adopted this approach to every life circumstance. We'd have a logical, tactical way to solve problems with a checklist made into law, bound into an approved manual, and available to reference at a moment's notice. Disagreements could easily be solved by referring to the manual. Whenever something goes awry, simply pull out a procedure that has a pre-established task list to be accomplished in the event of an emergency. This quick reference guide would be tabbed and easy to circumnavigate. Some checklists would be available in a written linear form. More complex issues would be written on an easy-to-follow flow chart.

Let's put my philosophy to the test.

You walk in the door and your wife is pissed because the dog took a shit on the new carpet. Rather than involving yourself in a verbal diatribe where no one wins, you simply consult the manual. A flow chart might look like this: Is the dog present? Yes or no. If yes, does the dog look ashamed? If yes, look out the window. Is the weather in an inclement state that might keep the dog from wanting to relieve itself outside? If no, is the doggie door working properly? If no, repair the doggie door. The chart would continue with detailed instructions on how to fix every possible problem that caused the doggie door malfunction. The guidelines would be followed, and the procedure completed. More likely than not, the checklist would have been studied and perhaps even memorized before the incident occurred. This would enable the individual to act quickly and confidently. What may be mistaken as egotism is just preparedness.

Once the procedure is successfully completed, there may be additional information gathered during a follow-up investigation. In an aeronautical situation, the pilot meets with ground crew, such as a mechanic or counselor to go over what happened in the air and to seek guidance as to how the problem developed and continue to trouble-shoot the glitch. This ensures the problem doesn't reoccur. If new information is discovered, it's added to the manual.

In the instance of the doggie door malfunction, fol-low-up investigations may include studies on the opera-tion of the doggie door, previous problems encountered with this type of doggie door, and past solutions that proved successful. Advanced classes would offer a deeper study into the dog's breed, age, tendencies, and potty-training history.

Pilot checklists usually only address issues that can be managed from inside the cockpit. If a solution to the problem would require the pilot to leave the flight deck, it's probably not on the checklist. Additionally, the checklist would not ask why you didn't remember to go to the hard-ware store last week to buy the springs needed to repair the doggie door in the first place. To be fair, a trip to the hardware store last week could have prevented the prob-lem; but asking the question does not provide a solution in the present circumstance. Checklists are written to simply identify a problem, produce a solution, and occasionally give guidance on how to implement the solution. Equally important, the checklist can help you reassess the solution to confirm it's still working.

Aviation checklists do not spend any time assessing blame. That is the job of the FAA and the pissed-off wife. The Federal Government has reached expertise level in spending years critiquing a decision that a pilot had three seconds to make. And while you may not have had anything to do with the dog poo on the carpet, you'd better believe that somehow spousal investigations will assess the blame to you.

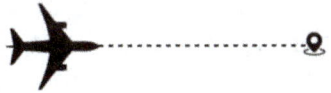

By nature, pilots are problem solvers. It's in the job description, right after *take the big machine full of people into the air and get them from Destination A to Destination B.* Pilots must think and act quickly. Solving problems is how we stay alive.

Imagine my surprise when I learned in a counselling session that not everyone is interested in having their problems solved. Some people just want you to listen to them. While I empathize with this philosophy, in my worldview, if problems aren't solved the plane goes down. If you have problems that you don't want solved, your best option is to talk to a dog. They are phenomenal listeners, and I know for a fact that they feel and care. They are incredibly content to absorb all your problems without making a single suggestion.

While there are no magic wands to wave over problems, most pilots would assert that magic is derived from understanding your environment. Understanding your environment allows you to produce Standard Operating Procedures that can prevent any number of problems. The wonderful thing about SOPs is that you can't argue with them. Each pilot is trained on the same SOPs, and no one is allowed to bring their own procedures into the cockpit.

I fantasize about a list of SOPs for relationships—

just envision the simplicity of this established life! Perhaps the next time I find myself furloughed, I will launch this innovative company, which will no doubt become a multi-billion-dollar business. This new business would serve individuals preparing to live as a family and produce a set of SOPs pertaining to their individual needs. Training would be required, and each family member would be instructed on their specific job in this environment. The company would set up personalized laws for each person, which would be agreed upon prior to cohabitation, and everyone would follow the laws. Periodically, family members would be tested on proper usage of the SOPs and regular drills on checklist execution would be mandatory.

SOPs could ensure a finely tuned morning routine each day with systems in place for every possible scenario. The list could include items such as coffee, breakfast, morning rituals, predetermined morning discussions, day planning, and departure time. Should any of these sequences hit a snag, family members would simply find the checklist appropriate to the situation and proceed.

Even an utter calamity like waking up to no coffee could be resolved with proper procedure. A checklist would lead the user through various ways to tackle this decaffeinated fiasco. A logical solution is almost predetermined with proper checklist usage. Is there water? Coffee grounds? Is the coffee making apparatus plugged into a working outlet? The reason the system works so well is that everyone involved in the operation would have a working knowledge of the coffee maker and the items required for making coffee. The checklist unpretentiously provides reinforcement should the emergency escalate.

It's just coffee, you may be thinking. Do we really need an SOP for coffee?

The lack of coffee prevents the progression of the day and the ability to accomplish duties. Suddenly important events requiring an on-time departure have been compromised. The snowball effect could easily confound the rest of the plans for the day, disrupting pleasant and peaceful family interactions. It's time for the emergency checklist, which has been tabbed in advance for easy navigation.

In addition to SOPs and checklists, pilots and crew members receive training in communication. My multibillion-dollar company would provide an extensive communication certification. You may need to explain to your family members that due to the coffee delay, morning rituals will need to be shortened to make a timely departure, providing that safety measures are not compromised. Effective communication, with the help of SOPs and checklists, removes emotion from the equation. Rather than causing CoffeeGate 2024 with hurtful words, you simply follow the communication checklist that ensures even without caffeine, you converse in a respectful and diplomatic manner to preserve familial bonds.

In the airline business, when the safety of other humans is at-stake, little things like feelings will need to be put at the bottom of the calculation. Once the plane is safely on the ground, there will be plenty of time to discuss hurt feelings and how someone's opinion was misconstrued. In fact, most SOPs require follow-up investigations that use differing opinions to determine better outcomes in the future.

There's more to *A Pilot's Guide to Successful Living* than just checklists and SOPs. Pilots must learn to delegate authority. Once you have delegated authority, you must respect the authority.

When a big airplane arrives at a gate, it takes approximately 20 people to get the plane ready for the next flight. There's no way the captain can personally oversee everything that needs done. He must trust the crew, the fuelers, the caterers, the cleaners, and the people hooking the airplane to the tug for push back. There must be a level of reliance on all the crew members.

Pilots don't work 9-5 jobs. They must leave their family units for days, sometimes weeks, at a time. If they are married, and especially if they have children, pilots must delegate their parenting and household responsibilities. Furthermore, they must trust the authority which they have delegated. Reentering a family unit after traveling, the properly trained pilot will offer support. Comments such as "Nice job," or "Thank you," are required. Any sort of comments that begin with, "That's not the way I would have done it," are not acceptable.

Pilots operate their careers through checklists and SOPs. At times, the lists seem overwhelming, but each has its place and purpose. Over the years, I've developed my own personal technique. First and foremost, fly the plane. Second, perform the first couple of checklist items by memory; and third, consult the checklist to ensure that all expectations and safety measures have been met.

How can this apply to happy everyday living?

When the pressures of life on the ground are mounting and becoming overwhelming, remember to fly the airplane first. That might mean quickly grabbing the vacuum cleaner and getting it running before a family member enters through the door. This refutes the perceived negatives of any napping, game playing, television watching, or simply sitting in silence and thinking of nothing. I used to have a dog named Benny who enjoyed sleeping on my chest during naps. He was an excellent alarm system and could detect a car coming up the driveway in plenty of time for me to grab the vacuum cleaner. I can't give up all my secrets, but that's a good one.

I'm now accepting investors for my aforementioned business idea. And with the extra money I've saved you on therapy expenses, might I suggest you head to your local animal shelter and adopt a loving mutt. No need to thank me, but feel free to buy an extra copy of this book and pass on the wisdom of *A Pilot's Guide to Successful* Living to whoever you think needs it most.

15

Chasing Sunsets

Chasing sunsets in a jet is a unique experience. As you climb westward into the sky, you can watch the sun slide down into a molten globule, majestically dipping below the horizon line. At around 40,000 feet you begin to see the curvature of the earth, how the horizon tucks back into itself, distant destinations impossible to see, hiding just behind the sphere. Once you reach altitude, the sun reemerges, almost as though it rose again briefly, only to descend again. Flying at this height you can observe a second sunset, this time not just below the horizon line, but also over the earth's arc, like a glowing ember fading into the distance.

Throughout my career, I've had the opportunity to chase many sunsets in many captivating and far off places. It's one of the joys of being a pilot. I like to say I've been everywhere twice; but I probably haven't seen as much as most people who've traveled as tourists to those locations. Sometimes my view of an area is only a bird's-eye glance as we land, then take off minutes or hours later. Other times, layover schedules have allowed me to explore. I've been to every state in the United States so many times I couldn't give you an estimate. I've flown to some of the most beautiful islands in the Caribbean, to the Spice Islands in Southeast Asia, picturesque cities in Europe, and to five of the seven continents. My passport bulged with expanded pages that had to be specially ordered when there was no room left to stamp.

But between all the travel and all the places, the flying sticks with me the most. And flying into Toncontín International Airport just outside of Tegucigalpa, Honduras, particularly stands out in my memory. Ranked by the History Channel as the second most extreme airport in the world, passengers have described the descent into this airport as a thrilling roller coaster ride. So many planes have crashed in the area that Hondurans have been known to cross their fingers and pray when they see a plane approach and applaud after a successful touchdown.

Surrounded by mountainous terrain, Toncontín's runway is unnaturally short. Thriving international hubs may have runways as long as 13,000 feet. Regional airports usually have the shortest runways, measuring between 3,000 and 6,000 feet. The runway into Honduras's capital city is just 6,000 feet. Since the runway is located at the base of a mountain, the construction of the airport required extreme measures. Part of a hill called Cerro Juana Laínez had to be leveled to allow for more wing space on the final approach. Special training procedures are required for new captains to fly into the airport, along with a mandatory video.

The conditions at Toncontín Airport are specialized enough that it can only be used during the daytime with a dry runway by experienced pilots. Inevitably, the management would ask what it would take to land a plane there at night in the rain. "Not much," I'd tell them. "Just find a young, inexperienced pilot. If you can find two, who are both starving to death, that would be preferable."

Since Toncontín Airport is only four miles from the heart of the capital, the airstrip is surrounded not only by mountains, but also by residential neighborhoods. Pilots must make a dramatic 45 degree turn after negotiating the updraft of all the elevations, and then touch the wheels into the bowl-shaped runway just moments later.

By the time I landed in Toncontín Airport the first time, I had confidence on my side. Personal trainers tell their clients that abs are built in the kitchen, not in the gym. Similarly, I started my preparation long before starting the plane's engines. Before taking off or landing at any airport, a pilot considers many things, from weather conditions to how much iguana poop is on the runway. Data is analyzed, numbers are calculated, and V-speeds are determined.

I was fortunate to accompany my crash pad buddy, Jeremy Miller, on his first descent into Toncontín. Giant clouds cast shadows over the rich verdant terrain, blanketing parts of the city with darkness. As we drew closer to the airport, the colorful Honduran houses rose up to greet us, sturdy neighborhoods built on unyielding earth. The runway wasn't immediately visible.

First, we had to make our 45-degree turn, and the plane wavered slightly as we bounced along the updrafts. As soon as the approach became visible, Jeremy said what goes through every pilot's mind when seeing it for the first time. "You've got to be shitting me."

By the time the runway was clearly visible through the cockpit, we were already well into our descent and caught in a laughing fit, the landing fast approaching. In the last moments before touching down, we were so low over residential areas that it appeared as though we'd decided to land on a city street, traffic rushing by right underneath us.

Without much time to contemplate the situation, the wheels touched down and I could hear the relieved laughter and heightened conversation through the cockpit door. Once we'd landed, it was like any other extreme ride.

"Let's do that again!" The challenge and thrill of landing at Toncontín never decreased in the many opportunities I had to fly into Honduras, and as someone who thrives at pushing the boundaries of what others may view as difficult, I loved it each and every time.

Never a person to collect souvenirs, I collected many memories instead. It's my opinion that if I need a material object to help me remember something, the memory probably doesn't rank high enough anyway. Unlike physical things, memories are a constant companion, require no luggage, take up no space, and are incredibly easy to share. But memories can be a slippery slope. The more you collect, the more you want to create.

One of my most vivid memories of flying was navigating into Haiti shortly after the January 12, 2010, earthquake that shook the small nation with a 7.0 magnitude on the Richter Scale. The event had catastrophic effects, triggering an unprecedented humanitarian crisis, killing more than 200,000 people, and leaving the government in shambles as it fought to rebuild not only buildings, but economic stability.

The airline I worked for at the time was given a FEMA code and a government contract to assist in the evacuation of American citizens out of Haiti. This trip is etched into my memory for many reasons, but perhaps the most significant is because I was accompanied by my son, Rob. The FEMA contract allowed us to fly under a different set of rules called public use. In simple terms this meant we could fudge some of the normal regulations due to the intense circumstances of the situation. Rob, who was 20 at the time and had just completed his EMT training, was allowed to ride in the jump seat under the public use laws.

We were one of the first airplanes to arrive after the disaster. Our initial mission was to drop off doctors and medical supplies and bring back as many U.S. citizens as possible, and then turn around and do it again. Without an air traffic control tower in operation, pilots were in charge of controlling the airspace, which is not uncommon in a non-towered airport, but almost unheard of with the number of planes coming and going to assist in disaster relief. Further complicating issues were the many military aircraft and non-English speaking pilots, all in the same traffic pattern.

Because of the tightness of the final approach, I made the decision to turn off the auto pilot and hand fly the jet to our destination. The autopilot disconnect signal on a *Boeing 737* is a siren. I turned around for a moment and caught a glimpse of my son's face. His eyes grew with the intensity of the siren. "It's okay," I told him. "This is normal."

We landed without complications, but what we found on the ground was anything but normal. A stench filled the air that could be experienced with multiple senses. This was a smell that reached out and touched you. It hung in the air with such density, you could almost see it. It smelled like passing a skunk or a rotting deer carcass on the side of the highway, only this smell settled in the back of your throat and didn't dissipate as you continued to drive. Disorganized fear and panic displayed itself on the faces of the frenzied relief workers. The military was doing its best, but with limited resources. One of their main tasks was to set up a temporary control tower to safely facilitate the evacuations. Lines of people formed, waiting for their chance to climb aboard the planes and escape to a safer, saner world.

Rob, despite his youth and inexperience in a natural

disaster zone, instinctively took on the job of organizing the removal of valuable medical equipment from the airplane. He later abandoned the jump seat to be with injured evacuees in the back, dealing with broken bones, lacerations, and trauma victims. As a father, it was an incredibly proud moment to see him excel in such an intense situation.

The amount of chaos we experienced on the ground in Haiti was like nothing I've seen before or since. At one point we were blocked from loading desperate passengers onto our plane because the TSA hadn't arrived yet. It was one of the few times in my life I was infuriated. Later there were stories of pilots who filled their planes with more passengers than there were seats available, passengers who had not been cleared by the TSA, who might or might not have been American citizens. Because of the regulations in place, there were planes that took off without record of the flight or the crew. The TSA in conjunction with the FAA launched an investigation that lasted for several years, but to my knowledge, nothing ever came from it.

The memories I collected from Haiti weren't the type that fueled my desire to collect more, but I carry them with me, nonetheless. I am proud of the work we were able to do, and the hope that an airplane can bring. Sometimes when I think about the terrorist attacks on 9/11, I'm dismayed at the destruction that was brought about by airplanes. It helps me to remember that when used correctly, airplanes bring the possibility to save lives, to transport people to safety, to bring needed life-preserving medical equipment into disaster areas. Those memories renew my love for airplanes.

All my life I've heard discussions about what a soul is. I'm not claiming I know, but I would guess it's the part that lives on after the body dies. If that's the truth, the soul must be the way you laughed, the way you moved, the effect you had on other people's lives. And I'd like to think that memories are somehow stored in your soul as well, that they continue to live on.

Most flights are uneventful with uncomplicated weather conditions to unmemorable, mundane locations. Other flights are memorable, not because of the flight, but because of your traveling companions and the journey's end. Sharing traveling adventures with my children probably tops my list of memories that I've collected and treasured.

Just before my daughter's thirteenth birthday, she was diagnosed with Type I childhood diabetes. This was an incredibly depressing and confusing time in my life, and I tortured myself wondering if we could have done something to prevent Katie's disease, or if I could do anything to facilitate a cure. At the time, I was completely ignorant about diabetes, and since this was before insulin pumps and other technological advances that have made the disease so much easier to manage, I catastrophized that she'd probably never again be able to eat anything that tasted good, and that travel was likely out of the question.

As I learned more about diabetes, I came to realize it wasn't a death sentence if carefully managed, and that most of the 1.6 million other Americans who had Type I diabetes seemed to be doing okay. Since I'm not a trained medical doctor, there was little I could do for Katie in the way of direct care other than driving her to appointments and making sure she had insulin. But being a typical dad, doing nothing wasn't an option. Most men like to fix things, and diabetes wasn't a problem I could fix. So I helped her in the way I knew best. I told her to plan a trip and we would go. As upset as I was over Katie's diagnosis,

I couldn't even imagine what she must have internalized at that young age. It was important that she knew she could still live her life; and I'd be right by her side.

Katie, who was a precocious child and now a brilliant adult, could never do anything on a small scale. Within hours and without use of the Internet, which had barely debuted at the time, Katie had a trip to London planned, seven days long and every hour filled. For me, going to London was nothing. I'd flown into Heathrow countless times. But traveling with my daughter, who was dealing with a brand-new health condition, was both special and stressful.

This time I didn't pilot the plane. Instead, Katie and I were non-revving, also known as non-revenue flying, which means flying for free as a perk of working for the airline. We were back in coach, about as far away from the cockpit as you could get. Somewhere in the middle of the Atlantic Ocean, Katie started asking me questions. "What time is it in Omaha? What time is it in London?" I realized she was trying to calculate her insulin injections to align with the new time zone. She figured it all out on her own.

For three days we played tourist. We rode the Tube and the double-decker buses. We walked across Westminster Bridge while hearing the chime of Big Ben ring. When we got too tired to walk, we simply hopped on one of the buses and rode the route from one end to the other, seeing the sights while catching our breath. I cherish the memory of when Katie turned to me and said, "I will always remember this, Dad." I also remember waking her up in the middle of the night, worried about her insulin levels. In a much less loving tone, she said, "Leave me alone." She was okay. She was managing her disease.

Katie had wanted to spend an entire day at Harrods Department Store, but when we stopped in the evening before for a quick preview, she decided that wasn't how she wanted to spend her day. We suddenly had 24 hours with no itinerary. So early the next morning, we rode the Tube to the train station, where we bought tickets on the Chunnel Train to Paris. We spent the day sightseeing. We saw the Eiffel Tower, the Champs-Élysées, the Arch de Triumph, the Louvre, and even the famous "The Thinker" statue in the Musée Rodin. I remember eating at a French café on the sidewalk and Katie commenting, "This is just like the movies." That night, we caught the last train back to the small Holiday Inn in London. I remember Katie saying, "It's good to be home, isn't it, Dad?"

While Rob escaped any big medical surprises before his thirteenth birthday, it seemed only fair that I offer him a trip of his choice since his sister got one. He wanted to go on a white-water rafting trip. Buena Vista, Colorado is known for its thrilling, unforgettable rafting tours and breathtaking scenic views; so we made that our destination. I told Rob we could fly into Denver and rent a car from there, or we could just drive straight from Omaha. He said, "Let's just drive." He went on to explain, "The car seats are more comfortable, we can listen to our own music and bring whatever we want. Why would we want to fly on an airplane since it's our vacation?" He's a man after my own heart, and to this day, I'll drive ten hours instead of ride the airlines for a lot of the reasons Rob gave at the young age of 13. We spent three days on the river and camped every night. It's still one of my best vacations ever.

Every parent enjoys the ability to teach their children, and when the kids actually appreciate learning something you've shared, you feel like you've conquered the universe. Traveling with family has offered glimpses of those happy moments. Both of my children love to travel and have been to many points on the globe; and I'd like to think exposing them to travel as children is a big reason for that.

I recollect a hotdog stand in Chicago; and as we placed our orders, I told Rob to order it "Chicago-style". He did; and he loved it. The Chicago dog comes with everything–peppers, sauerkraut, mustard, onions, relish, and a slice of pickle--but it doesn't come with ketchup. It's considered a sin to put ketchup on a Chicago-style dog. It can get you kicked out of a hotdog stand if you ask for ketchup. We were in Chicago as a family to attend a speech that Katie had been asked to give to a group of her colleagues. I remember the speech was a bit over my head. A few academic types were nodding along; they must have understood it. Those of us without advanced degrees in neuropsychology, i.e.: all of our family except for Katie, sat in the audience providing all the respect and dignity that Katie deserved. I can't prove it, but I know we were all thinking about that hotdog stand and wondering how far away it was from the venue, and how soon the speech would be over so we could go order another Chicago-style dog.

After being on the road for several days, you look forward to being home. It's a funny part of being a pilot. Most people want to leave their homes to go on vacation, while I just wanted to go home for mine. Everything about home starts to sound wonderful–your family, friends, your own bed, home cooking, and your dogs. There's a contented pleasure in knowing exactly what's around the next corner of your neighborhood, a tranquility in the absence of surprise. There's nothing more exciting than knowing exactly what's going to happen on Wednesday night at 7 o'clock.

Upon returning from a long trip, I enjoy digging through my T-shirt drawer, having just worn the same few shirts over and over again while traveling. The uniform makes it simple to pack, but putting on the same shirt and pants day after day gets old.

A simple indulgence in being at home is consistency. Simple things like waking up and going to bed at the same time, a familiar and memorized path to the bathroom, knowing the exact spot on the shower handle for the proper temperature–these are small luxuries often taken for granted. Everyone has experienced the phenomenon of waking up in the morning, not sure of where you are. It takes a second for the brain to reorganize itself. At home, this rarely happens. The brain awakes, sure of its surroundings; and that is a form of restfulness that's hard to describe to someone who doesn't travel for a living.

Over the years I've learned a lot about professional communication, but by the time I figured out communication in my personal life it was too little, too late. Walking in the door from a trip and hearing the words, "Let's go out to a restaurant to celebrate that you're home," sounds exciting to every member of the family, but me. Knowing what I know now, instead of saying, "Oh my God, another restaurant?" my pre-rehearsed communication strategy would cue me to say, "Sounds great! Let's go to Chuck E. Cheese. A noisy environment surrounded by strangers is exactly where I would enjoy a meal tonight." While I was gone working, my wife was single-parenting, cooking all the meals, and doing all the bedtime routines. She likely needed an escape from the monotony that I craved.

For most people, traveling is a once-in-a-lifetime adventure. For me, it's a fortunate job that has allowed me many unforgettable experiences. As you do anything over and over, you learn some tricks. I've learned to pack lightly, have a back-up plan, and relax.

Unfortunately, travel has lost some of its charm over the years. It used to be that each destination was unique, each with its own charm. There used to be an airport around Quincy, Illinois, that had a small round terminal built entirely out of native rocks. The restaurant inside was run by an old guy who didn't have a menu. You ate what he decided to cook that day. Though I was only there twice, I still remember that the beef stew was phenomenal. The second time, I had a pork tenderloin sandwich that I've yet to duplicate either in size or taste.

There was a small airport in Indianola, Mississippi, with only a couple of plastic chairs to sit on; and the building looked like it hadn't been cleaned since its construction. Catfish farming was the main industry in the area. I loved going down to watch the little catfish drive the tractors, pull the plows, and plant the catfish food. The biggest problem was, quite often, the fish would slide right off the tractor seat. The only restaurant close by was an antique store with a woman who cooked for her clients. Somehow, we found out about it, and she invited us for lunch one day. She served us fried catfish, catfish pâté, and a chocolate cream pie. I would crawl back on my hands and knees to eat that meal again.

There was a seafood restaurant in Russellville, Arkansas. I don't remember the name of the restaurant, but I remember the item on the menu. It was called the boatload, which was all the fresh seafood catch of the day that could fit onto a plate. Before the waitress even had a chance to set down a menu, I said, "I'll take the boatload, please."

Omaha, Nebraska, is famous for steaks; most people have heard of the Omaha Steaks brand name. My favorite butcher shop in Omaha is a small, independent operator whose motto is, "People who work for Omaha

Steaks come here for steak."

When I write too close to lunchtime, my memories circulate around food, but I have been to many other places where eating was not the main objective. Back in my running days, there was a park close to the Dayton Ohio, airport. The park featured a beautiful three-mile trail that meandered over bridges, through tunnels, over small streams, and up and down hills through a canopy of trees. Even on the hottest days, it was a cool run.

I've spent hundreds of days in Washington, D.C., but have only skimmed the surface of all that the Smithsonian has to offer. A recent trip to Boise, Idaho, gave me new appreciation for the vast beauty of the Rocky Mountains, the Canadian side of the Rockies being much less populated and always spectacular. I've seen the purple mountain majesties and the shining seas, and walked on some of the most pristine beaches in the world—Destin, Florida, ranking towards the top. The beaches there look like sugar poured right up against the clear blue water.

Nude beaches are a sight to see; I'd recommend the one in Hialeah, Florida. There's not much to say about nude beaches, other than all the women running scared away from me. What most people don't understand about nude beaches is they are mostly filled with a bunch of old people that no one would want to see naked anyway. But it's a little like golf: out of every ten swings, there's that one shot that keeps a person coming back.

But there's been a sad trend I've noticed over the years. I remember Kansas City International Airport boasting such unique architecture, with three separate round terminals and buses that transported people between them. On a recent trip through the airport I saw the round terminals had been torn down and replaced by a terminal that looks like all the other airports in the country. Now when you're in Kansas City, you could just as easily close your eyes and open them and think you're in Tampa, or Detroit, or Minneapolis.

The trip from the airport to the hotel has also become disappointing. There's a Walgreens on one side of the street, a McDonald's on the other, and 14 Starbucks coffee shops next to the Hilton Garden Inn with architecture identical to every city. I used to say you could blindfold me and put me somewhere in the middle of the United States, and within minutes, I could tell you where I'm at. I could not do that today. Everything looks the same.

It's not just the airports or the hotels. The airplanes, the cars, trucks, and most of the people even look the same.

Once when I was in Guayaquil, Ecuador, we had several hours to kill and some of the flight attendants wanted to go shopping. It would require leaving and re-clearing customs, which always bore the chance of someone not making it back in time for the flight. I'd been flying with my friend, David Samaroo, who told the flight attendants, "Do you see that *747* over there? That's a freight company. Everything you could find in those stores just came in that airplane from Miami."

16

Travel Tips, or the Least Amount of Crazy

Packing Essentials

As a professional traveler, I have often been asked for travel tips. And the question foremost on people's minds seems to be, "What should I pack?"

I've seen people with suitcases so big my little sister could probably crawl inside and fit nicely. When I see those people, I'm the one with the questions. *Do they have anything left in their house? Did they really just pay the exorbitant oversized baggage fee? And are they aware that the airlines sometimes lose human organs in transport, and do they really want to take a chance with what must surely be all of their worldly possessions?*

I've also traveled with people who wear one shirt all week.

Somewhere in the middle is the least amount of crazy.

Whether I'm traveling for two days or two months, I pack pretty much the same: toiletries, a pair of jeans, four or five pairs of underwear and socks, workout shorts, a few T-shirts, and a good pair of running shoes. I'd rather find a laundry room and wash my clothes every week, rather than carry around three weeks' worth of clothes.

At this stage in my life, it would take a tremendous effort to convince me I needed to wear a suit or tie; but if circumstances changed while I was on the road, I'd probably just wander down to the local Salvation Army, buy what I needed, wear it to the event, and then leave it in the hotel room for the next needy soul.

Some people are filled with anxiety, worried they forgot something. But there are only a few things that cannot be forgotten: your ID, wallet, and phone. Everything else you can buy at Walmart.

A good rule of thumb is, if you can't lift it into the overhead compartment, you probably don't need it. Something happens to otherwise-intelligent humans when they step aboard an airplane. Before boarding, they likely saw at least half a dozen metal baskets with signs that read, "If your carry-on doesn't fit in this container, it won't fit in the overhead compartment." But at no point did they consider the message might be directed at them. Airports must cause people to lose all sense of spatial reasoning because I can't tell you how many people I've seen attempt to shove their oversized bag into an overhead compartment, get it stuck halfway, and then block the aisle for the rest of the boarding passengers. You've likely been trapped behind the guy while he grunts, sweats, and curses, shoving against hope that his square bag will fit into the round hole. If the bag miraculously squeezes in, I wonder how the hell he expects to get it back out again.

One time, a woman boarded my flight with a miniature horse as her carry-on. To be fair, it was actually a therapy animal, and it was about the size of a German Shepherd. The woman was blind and crippled, and the horse was strong enough to keep her upright. The whole situation was absolutely fascinating. She told me the horse was smart and easy to train. I could have spent all day asking her questions, but for some reason it didn't occur to me to ask her how she went about potty-training a horse. Honestly, the horse was so cute that I would have let it poop in the back of my plane.

Navigating Airport Security

I also get questions about how to get through the security lines quickly. This one is pretty simple: know the rules and follow them. Don't buy a $45 cup of double espresso mocha java pumpkin spice latte with a vanilla cold foam and then act shocked when you can't bring it through security. While it's somewhat humorous to watch someone attempt to chug 42 ounces of steaming hot coffee, you really don't want to be the person waiting behind them. This may come as a surprise to some, but you can buy coffee on the other side of security. Do everyone else a favor and wait until you are through screening before you indulge your caffeine addiction.

Another way to quicken security screening is to dress for success. Leave the belt at home, don't wear giant-ass metal earrings, and choose clothes that are free of heavy ornaments. The TSA agents will always ask the same questions. Is there anything in your pockets? Did you remove your jacket? It seems like every time I'm at the airport, I'm forced to witness the multiple-walk-through scenario. A big cowboy will walk through the metal detectors; it'll beep, and he'll get sent back. Then he removes his huge belt buckle. He'll make another attempt, and it'll beep again. Turns out he had a pocketknife he'd forgotten about. Back through again. Beep. Wouldn't you know that his shirt is bedazzled with metal buttons?

And God help you if you get behind someone with multiple piercings. It's an awkward experience to stand in line, waiting for a guy to remove his tongue ring.

Strollers have to be folded, so it'll quicken your process if you remove your kid before trying to flatten the contraption down to a size that'll squeeze through the security scanner. Though I honestly saw a dad stick his kid into one of the security bins once. The kid was happily babbling away, as the conveyor belt drew him closer to the gaping hole of the x-ray machine. I'm not sure if the dad thought his kid needed to be scanned, or if he was just trying to keep the kid out of trouble for a few moments.

Quality Nutrition on the Go

Surprisingly, not a lot of people have come to me for diet advice. They must not know that under this layer of pudge, my body is basically exactly like Superman's. But as someone who has traveled frequently, I am aware of the concerns and trials of maintaining a healthy diet when away from home.

Crew meals used to be excellent, tasty, healthy, and professionally prepared. At some point, the quality degraded to peanuts and candy. Most airlines pay crews perdiem on the road. In most cases, it's enough money to either make healthy choices away from home, or to make your car payment that month. But not both. Healthy choices are not cheap.

Let's say you find a Wendy's in the airport, and you've been allocated $20 for lunch. You could choose the apple pecan salad, which is one of the lowest calorie full-meal menu items available at the restaurant. The cost for this salad is $10.39 and will likely not cause an immediate heart attack; as a bonus, it only has 550 calories. You can feel good about this, but if you are thirsty and you want to keep your calorie count minimal, you'd better add on another $3 for a bottle of water. Compare this to the Baconator™, which as indicated by the name, is loaded with bacon, so will obviously taste a whole lot better than the sad salad option. Besides, remember all those Salmonella outbreaks a few years back that were associated with lettuce? *Perhaps*, your brain starts to tell you, *the Baconator™ is truly the healthier choice.* And this is before you compare the cost. The Baconator™ combo, which comes with fries and a drink, costs only $9.60. Sure, the burger alone has more than 1,000 calories, and if you start to add in the calories of the fries and the drink, it just gets depressing. But you've saved almost $4, and you probably won't be hungry again in 45 minutes. Sure, a few too many Baconators™ could lead you to a heart attack, but who wants to die from Salmonella?

At home I eat healthily. In the grocery store, I have lots of willpower. But get me 500 miles away from home, and my mind no longer recognizes calories. These days I'm no longer tied to per-diem food allotments, but on the road with an expense account, I have often been ashamed of myself.

Here's a tip I've found helpful when traveling: calories count; so count the calories. Let's say you need breakfast. If you were at home, it would be easy enough to pull some frozen vegetables out of the freezer and make a nice, low-calorie omelet packed with nutrients. But since you don't have access to a kitchen or likely a freezer full of smart options, you have to purchase breakfast instead. You could go to IHOP and get a stack of pancakes, which everyone can agree is a typical American breakfast option. But before you pour that syrup, you'd better log 800 calories, 160 grams of carbohydrates, and 40 grams of sugar. Keep in mind, this is a stack of pancakes without syrup or toppings of any kind, which is pretty unrealistic. Your better, healthier option is to buy a bag of Ho Hos. These Hostess brand delicacies have only 270 calories, just 38 grams of carbohydrates, and a measly 26 grams of sugar. Best of all, no high-calorie syrup is needed.

If you think about it, both pancakes and Ho Hos are made with flour, eggs, and sugar; so they are basically equivalent breakfast choices. It just so happens that Ho

Hos are the healthier option. As a bonus, they are easily portable and packable, which is a lot more than can be said about pancakes.

Hotel Etiquette

I know something about hotels. In my career, I've stayed in thousands of hotel rooms. If you get to pick, I recommend choosing a room between the third and seventh floors. The first and second floors are fairly easy to break into; and escaping a fire gets trickier once you pass the seventh floor. That being said, I still love the top floors for the views.

When staying in a fancier hotel, it's good to maintain a certain level of decorum. My friend, Bruce Clark, and I flew together a lot and shared a crash pad in Chicago. Once, we checked into a nice hotel in Phoenix. Our rooms were about 20-yards apart on opposite sides of a lovely garden. A charming rock bed and a colorful flower box adorned the front of my room. Bruce and I were both behind our prospective closed doors when I got an idea. I came out and removed one of the rocks from the garden. Using one of the baseball-throwing techniques that Bruce had tried to teach me, I aimed for Bruce's door, and it hit with a loud thwack. I ducked back inside and peeked out my window.

Bruce came out, looked around outside his room, shrugged his shoulders and went back inside.

Of course, I immediately grabbed another rock and managed to hit his door a second time. Again, Bruce came out. This went on several more times until finally I heard Bruce yell from across the garden, "Osborn! I know you're out there and I know you're doing this, and I'm not opening the door anymore!"

Wearing nothing but the hotel bathrobe, I opened the door and chastised my friend. "Bruce, quiet down. This is a nice place, and I don't want you to get us kicked out of here." I think he really appreciated being the recipient of my wisdom on the topic of hotel etiquette. From that point on, we would say, "If you need anything, just rock my door."

If you are ever in a hotel when you hear a fire alarm, grab your key and get out immediately. That being said, one night I was staying in a hotel room on the first floor with my family, including our two young children and our dog. We'd had a power failure at home, and since we were in the middle of one of Nebraska's bitter cold spells, we had no choice but to check into a hotel to avoid freezing to death. In the middle of the night, when the temperatures had dropped below zero, the fire alarm went off. Knowing that cold weather can sometimes trigger false alarms, I suggested to my family that we stay in the room. I also knew that cold weather could cause fires, but having experienced below-zero Nebraska winter nights before, I figured I'd take my chances burning to death.

My advice was not respected by the rest of the family. Fair enough. I remember sitting in my warm ground-floor room, making faces at my wife and kids who were shivering out in the cold. If the window had opened wide enough, I would have let them crawl back in.

Hampton Inns are usually very clean and well-kept, but the only good breakfast day at a Hampton Inn is bacon day. I've never cracked the code on when to anticipate bacon day. It always seems to be the day before I arrive or the day after I leave. But if they don't have bacon during your stay, there's probably a vending machine somewhere in the hotel where you can buy Ho Hos.

Hotel restaurants are generally marginal. Customers are often just passing through and unlikely to return; but a food service must be provided, so a lackadaisical effort is made. I've found delivery options near hotels to be excellent.

If you manage not to die in a hotel fire, be sure to collect points. You can trade these in for even more hotel stays where you can employ my helpful tips. Right now, I have enough Hilton points to keep myself in free rooms for several vacations, and enough points left over for just as many free breakfasts. But then again, it's never bacon day.

The Chatty Seat Mate

I've also been asked how to handle a chatty seatmate on the airplane. Normally the best thing to do is pull out a book, but this doesn't always deter the most extroverted of friendlies. Pretending you don't understand the language is a risk because you might end up with a polyglot next to you, which would just invite more conversation and result in an embarrassed admittance that you only speak English and a little bit of Pig Latin. In this day-and-age, if your reading attempt has failed you could always start coughing and blowing your nose, initiating a conversation with your seatmate along the lines of, "Hey, what are the symptoms for Covid again?" That'll probably keep them quiet. And it'll likely cause them to scoot farther away from you, providing you with extra space.

If you are a pilot and wearing your full uniform in the back of the plane, expect unwanted attention. Invariably, someone will come up to you and say, "Shouldn't you be at the front of the plane?" This will be followed by hysterical laughter; and you will grit your teeth, and pretend that you haven't already heard that joke 9,352 times. Usually I just say, "I'm going to land the plane back here on my iPad."

Just Relax

If you follow all these travel trips, you'll soon be traveling like a seasoned pro. But I've saved the most important tip for last, and it just so happens to be the same advice I gave my daughter on her wedding day. Relax, relax, and relax.

Airports are filled with people who are stressed, in a hurry, and pissed off. Traveling is not unlike your wedding day. There are high expectations, but it's not going to be a perfect day. There will be things that go wrong. But regardless of the unexpected curveballs or rocks slamming into your hotel door, the day will be fun and enjoyable.

It's important to remember that traveling can be stressful and laborious. If your expectation is that traveling will leave you rested, recharged, and ready for work, then you might want to adjust your expectations. Allocate a few days after your trip to simply relax on your couch. It's essential to recognize that travel can be demanding, so giving yourself time to unwind can make a significant difference.

In the convoluted world of airports and hotels, the quirks of fellow travelers, and the unpredictable nature of journeys, one truth remains constant: travel is as much about the unexpected detours as it is about the planned routes. So, the next time you find yourself stuck behind a passenger attempting to remove her belly button ring or having to make the choice between a salad and a bag of Ho Hos, take a deep breath, smile at the absurdity of the situation, and choose the Ho Hos. In the end it's not about the perfect trip; it's about the imperfect, beautiful, and utterly human experiences that make travel a profound and enriching part of our lives.

17

Blue Skies, Red Tape

One consistent question I've been asked throughout my life as an airline pilot is "What's it like to fly one of those big things?"

A basic airliner model produces roughly 28,000 pounds of thrust on takeoff. There's no exact formula, but that's approximately the power of ten locomotives. On takeoff, a fully-loaded plane can easily climb 3,000 feet per minute at sea level. For perspective, the world's tallest building, the Burj Khalifa in Dubai, doesn't even reach 3,000 feet into the sky. At altitude, the plane can cruise close to Mach .8, meaning 80-percent of the speed of sound. That's a great deal faster than the muzzle velocity of a .38 caliber revolver.

So, let's review. When I'm flying an airliner, I am more powerful than a locomotive. I can leap tall buildings in a single bound. And I'm faster than a speeding bullet. It's a bird! It's a plane! It's . . .

Well, actually, yes, it is a plane.

Flying a large airliner can actually be easier than flying a small aircraft. Larger jets have more automation to assist the pilot and *Boeing* jetliners have hydraulic-assisted controls, comparable to power steering in a car. Artificial feel systems built into flight control provide pilots with tactile feedback, or artificial sensations, which are important to give pilots a realistic sense of how the plane is behaving. This becomes especially important as you reach higher speeds and altitudes because the sensitivity of standard non-assisted flight controls also increases. Without the artificial feel, the controls would be too sensitive for humans to handle smoothly.

If all systems are functioning correctly when flying a large jet, the controls require only a slight pressure and finesse, rather than physically maneuvering the aircraft. No physical strength or endurance is required. However, in the event of a hydraulic system failure, the pilot would need to exert up to 70 pounds of pressure until it was possible to navigate to the nearest airport. To get an idea of what this feels like, the next time you are in a grocery store, grab one of those huge bags of dog food and carry it around while you do the rest of your shopping.

I've flown without the hydraulic assist many times ... in the simulator. This is a regular part of training. It takes a great deal of concentration to keep your mental faculties functioning while your body is feeling the torture of 70 pounds pushing back at you. The required regulation uniform shirt is almost always soaked-through at the end of this exercise.

The one time I experienced hydraulic system failure in an actual airplane was short and almost uneventful. I've always said the most dangerous part of flying is the drive to the airport. Part of what makes flying such a safe travel option is the amount of redundancy built into modern aircraft. The system redundancy includes backups for crucial functions such as multiple methods to deploy the landing gear or backup systems for maintaining cabin pressurization.

When something does go wrong in a large airplane, such as a hydraulic system failure, the pilot's knowledge and understanding of the backup systems becomes crucial.

While today's technology is advanced and includes redundant systems, it still relies on a skilled pilot to manage emergencies effectively. Technology cannot think for itself during a crisis, at least not yet. And until it does, the plane still needs a pilot.

There may come a day when pilots are part of the redundancy. Modern autopilot systems on today's big jets can already do almost everything, from executing a descending approach to facilitating a smooth landing. The modern airliner can even apply the brakes by itself. Furthermore, in contemporary corporate aircraft, cutting-edge technology exists that can enable a properly trained passenger to take control in case of pilot incapacitation. By simply pressing a designated button, the aircraft can automatically navigate to the nearest suitable airport and execute a safe landing.

In the recent past, it was customary for pilots to hand-fly the big jets until reaching altitude, engage the autopilot, and then disengage it again at descent to manually control the aircraft during the approach and landing phase. Today, it's not at all uncommon for the autopilot to turn on at 400 feet off the ground and stay on until after landing, provided there are no extenuating circumstances. The next time you are sitting in the back of the plane and wondering about your pilot's qualifications, you should probably be wondering about the qualifications of the plane's autopilot instead. The plane is likely flying itself.

When I was still flying the big jets, I frequently opted for hand-flying over autopilot. The decision was motivated by multiple factors, the sheer enjoyment of manual flying being number one. It also served as a way to maintain and sharpen my pilot skills. Furthermore, it also kept me prepared should a malfunction or emergency necessitate manual takeover.

Emergencies are few and far between. Today, the

modern airliner is so reliable that even in abnormal situations, crises seldom occur. Progressive maintenance prevents almost all unforeseen circumstances; parts are replaced based on how many hours of flight time they've had, rather than how well they are working. Most planes are checked daily and after each landing. Systems in the airplane can communicate with maintenance workers on the ground if something isn't working perfectly. Upon landing, the mechanic will be waiting at the gate with the necessary equipment, standing by for the replacement.

One undeniable perk of working as an airline pilot is the office space. It may not have the largest square footage, but the view cannot be duplicated. Looking out the flight deck windows is one of the sheer pleasures that doesn't get old no matter how long I fly. In just one three-hour flight, I can point out Devil's Tower in Wyoming, Lake Tahoe outside of Reno, and The Three Sisters in Washington state.

Not only is the view better in the cockpit, but so are the seats. As opposed to flying as a passenger, the cockpit chairs are fairly comfortable in the approximately 100-square-foot area. While the seats don't go back far enough to recline, they're easy enough to adjust for personal preferences. There's even a bar at the bottom of the instrument panel above the rudders where you can put up your feet and rest.

Though not everyone would enjoy sharing 100-square-feet with a co-worker, I thrive on the many at-altitude conversations I've had with flying partners over the years. Dialogue is an excellent distraction to keep you aware, awake, and involved. I believe pilots have solved many of the world's problems during these cockpit conferences, coming up with answers requiring advanced thinking and detailed planning. On long flights, even pilots with average intelligence suddenly become genius scientists in the thin air of elevation; though once we've landed, the implementation of our masterminds seems to slip out of the cabin doors as soon as they are open.

I've been asked if the extended periods I've spent at high altitudes have had any unusual effects on me. Outside of my superhuman capabilities that I've been contracted by the government to keep secret, there haven't been any discernible consequences. I do believe that spending so much of my life in close quarters with every virus known and unknown to mankind will probably allow me to live to be 120. I have to go back to grade school to recall the last time I was truly sick, though this might come as a surprise to some of the schedulers I've worked with over the years. Even though I've enjoyed remarkable health, I have perhaps called in a few 'sick days' in pursuit of 'schedule enhancement.' It's probably best if we keep this section just between us.

To quote Superman, "Dreams lift us up and transform us into something better." So, what's it like to fly one of those big machines? I guess I'd have to say transforming. It's humbling to wield such power and to perform superhuman feats that 150 years ago were thought to be impossible. I'd also have to say that though flying is mostly technical and almost always by the book, it's a whole lotta fun.

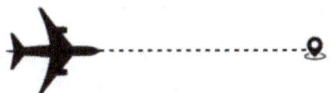

A cliche trope in books and movies is to show a scene where the pilot has a heart attack, and the passengers have to band together to figure out how to land the airplane. Thanks to co-pilots, there are very few instances where the flying public would be asked to come into the flight deck and save the day with whatever knowledge they've gained from flight simulator video games.

However, this brings me to another excellent question which I've often been asked, "Who pre-checks the pilot?"

Pilots are required to take a physical ever y six months with an FAA-certified doctor; and historically, the bar has been set high. Pilots can lose their license for a variety of ailments, including chronic conditions like diabetes, cardiovascular disease, and neurological disorders. It makes sense that someone with a history of substance abuse could be disqualified to receive a license, and someone with severe epilepsy or a seizure disorder would have a difficult time safely operating an aircraft. But until recently, pilots weren't able to even whisper words like sleep apnea or hypertension around an FAA doctor. Most pilots I know would ignore chest pain out of fear of losing their license. The thought of not flying was scarier than a heart attack.

A teacher will probably feel comfortable talking to a doctor about depression or about feeling groggy in the morning, but a pilot wouldn't dream of telling the flight doctor such a thing. Mental health disorders usually disqualify pilots. As a passenger, you would not feel relaxed knowing that your pilot had schizophrenia, even if he was having one of his good days. Certain mental health diagnoses should disqualify a pilot from operating an aircraft. But when stringent regulations keep pilots from discussing anxiety or mild obsessive-compulsive behaviors with medical professionals, we've gone a step too far. In fact, ignoring minor ailments can lead to bigger and more serious problems.

In October 2023, an off-duty pilot, Joseph Emerson, was charged with 83 counts of attempted murder when he tried to shut down a plane's engines while riding in the jump seat on a Horizon Air flight. Emerson, who'd suffered from a major bout of depression, later admitted to self-medicating with magic mushrooms following the death of a close friend. Instead of seeking medical help as his wife suggested, he told her, "Sarah, I can't be out of work. We have to pay a mortgage. If I go do that, I have to go through all these other hoops ... and we can't afford to do that."

What do normal people do when they suffer depression? Do normal people ever get stiff joints? What do normal people think if they need minor surgery or have a hernia? These are the questions I've often asked. Pilots usually ignore these minor ailments and continue flying.

FAA medical clearance has been called 'onerous and outdated' by many pilots and aviation experts. Especially in regard to mental health, FAA policies have hurt more than help. A 2006 study found that 12.6-percent of airline pilots had depression; and 4.1-percent reported suicidal thoughts in the previous two weeks. Because admitting to even mild depression or anxiety can put a pilot's license at-risk, many airline pilots simply avoid seeking help for highly treatable ailments. Researchers report that while hundreds of pilots suffer from depressive disorders, few seek treatment.

The FAA asks pilots to self-report medical issues. If a pilot were to admit he's seeking therapy or treatment for a mental health ailment, he would be pulled from flight status. And returning to work is no easy task. A pilot must regain medical clearance to fly, and this takes a full-fledged acrobatic performance to jump through all the hoops, which can take months or years. It makes sense that someone might want to take their chances with a magic mushroom rather than face the scrutiny of government oversight.

Federal policies are so invasive, that pilots are required to submit their therapist's notes to the FAA. Additionally, if a psychiatrist were to prescribe one of the five approved serotonin reuptake inhibitors, pilots must wait six months before they can reapply for medical clearance. Once they go off the medication, there's an additional sixty-day waiting period before reapplying.

Perhaps even more devastating, the FAA-mandated steps for reapplying are not covered by insurance. It can cost thousands to get all the required tests, evaluations, and specialist visits; and while all this is happening, the pilot is grounded with no income. It's downright disgraceful that pilots must choose between mental health and feeding their family. Politicians can pop a Zoloft without a second thought; yet they pass laws which keep pilots trapped in the Middle Ages of mental health, where a touch of anxiety might as well be a demon that needs exorcized. Mental health is no longer the taboo subject it once was; and yet, the FAA's laws are as antiquated as bloodletting.

A smart pilot will have a personal doctor not associated with the FAA. One of the first questions a pilot will ask his personal doctor is, "Is this on the record?" In fact, many pilots choose to pay for a doctor or therapist out of pocket in order to avoid insurance claims, which leaves a paper trail.

When I was a young boy, I used to pray that I would never have to wear glasses. Back then, glasses were enough to disqualify you from commanding an airplane. Today I wear glasses to drive or fly at night and to read really small print. Is it normal to wonder if I'm going to hell now that my eyes need a little help?

The FAA-mandated health screenings are less about keeping pilots healthy, and more about checking a box. Rather than encouraging transparency for healthier, fitter pilots, the system encourages pilots to hide ailments and suffer the consequences. In my opinion, it's a broken system that needs a complete overhaul. But for the foreseeable future, this is one more load of heavy cargo that transforms the magic of flying into a burdensome job.

18

Crew Chronicles

If you ever went to summer camp as a child, you may have some context of the relationships that can form between crew members in the airline world. You throw a bunch of strangers together, cut them off from their usual friends and family, provide them with shared experiences and inside jokes, feed them the same food, and have them sleep in close proximity to each other, and by the end of the week, close friendships have formed.

Some of my best friends are fellow pilots, and it's no wonder with the countless hours that we've spent together in close quarters.

I've worked with crew members of every age, race, religion, gender, sexuality, political party, dietary restriction, and personal hygiene preference. Perhaps the antidote to our country's division, spurred by social media and quick judgements, is to place individuals of different backgrounds together in a cockpit for several hours with nothing to do but fly a plane and converse. Given the expensive number of hours of training that would require, I suppose a long car ride across the country would work just as well. World peace would be within our grasp if we would step away from the screens and instead seek face-to-face relationships with others, engage in meaningful conversations, and get to know people on deep levels, rather than skimming over the surface and pronouncing a verdict.

When you are stuck in an enclosed space with another person, whether a stranger or a close friend, boredom will eventually kick in. I've discussed everything with my fellow coworkers, including all the things that you shouldn't bring up at a dinner party, but because we are managing an airplane, we have to listen and seek understanding rather than punch each other's lights out. This isn't to say that I've befriended every person I've ever flown with. The truth is, some people are just assholes, but more on that later.

I remember flying with my boss on one occasion; we had worked for a couple of different airlines together, and I considered him a friend, as I'm sure he did me. Our conversation took an unexpected turn toward his family, and he shared the painful experience of discovering his wife in bed with another woman. He'd had suspicions of clandestine endeavors happening behind his back, so one morning he got up, dressed in his uniform, packed his flight bag, and instead of leaving for the airport, he went out to breakfast at a restaurant. He came home unannounced, only to discover his wife's betrayal.

At the time I was not such a man of the world and found myself a bit dumbfounded. Looking back, I wish I had offered sympathy, or that I had at least asked a better question than the one that slipped out: "What did she look like?" He confided that finding your wife in bed with another woman is not as exciting as the immature man's mind might imagine. Instead, it was deeply emasculating and left him feeling mostly hopeless because there's no way to compete.

The camaraderie among professional airline crews is truly unique. It's astonishing how I can step into the cockpit alongside a complete stranger and, in as little as 15 minutes, smoothly operate an aircraft together in a professional and safe manner. This speaks volumes about the quality of the modern-day training we receive and underscores the unwavering level of professionalism we must maintain throughout our days, weeks, and months of flying.

Whether I find myself flying with a dear old friend I've known for years, an individual I don't particularly get along with, or a new first-time acquaintance, I firmly believe our level of professionalism should remain constant, unaffected by personal feelings. We continue to operate the aircraft, no matter the presence of any personality conflicts.

Certainly, nothing bonds crew members like shared experiences. Over the years, Suzanne Pheanis and I flew on many airlines together. Had we both been normal people, we may not have hit it off so well. One particularly memorable trip cemented our friendship. During a layover in Reno, I asked her to accompany me to Carson City, Nevada. I hadn't returned to this childhood haunt since I'd flown away with my mom and siblings all those decades ago; but since it housed my earliest childhood memories, I itched to see it again.

On the car ride, I told Suzanne all about the bright blue school where I attended kindergarten. I told her I still couldn't comprehend why my mom thought it was okay for me to walk all the way to school unaccompanied. After all, I was only in kindergarten, and the school was a mile's walk if it was an inch.

We found the school first, but it was no longer bright blue. I doubted my own memory as we stepped out of the car and walked around the building for a closer look. The bricks gleamed white in the afternoon sunlight; and when I was certain no one else was around, I used my thumbnail to scrape away a peeling piece of paint from the side of a brick. The flaky paint chip floated to the ground and revealed the bright blue color I so vividly remembered.

With that small piece of paint dislodged, I felt bowled-over by the long-forgotten childhood memories. They rushed back into my mind, surprising me with emotions that had been as carefully camouflaged as the color of the school. I remembered running home each day when the final bell rang, immediately asking my mom to tie a towel around my neck so I could play Superman. I remember her busy hands, taking a break from all the caretaking of my three younger siblings, pausing to knot the towel gently around my neck. Faster than a speeding bullet, I was out the door, imagining that I could fly up to the stars and see through walls. With that towel around my neck, I was the strongest boy in the world.

Suddenly, I remembered an older girl in the neighborhood who sometimes let me ride her big two-wheeler. Even though it was a girl's bike, I felt so grown up, standing to pedal, watching the big wheels carry me across the pavement. The girl also owned a horse nearby, and we'd go together to feed it carrots and apples.

Standing by the school, I could almost hear the songs playing on my mom's hi-fi set. Teresa Brewer, Elvis, and the Singing Nun Records—nearly audible memories that transported me back into the living room, imagining my bare toes on the worn carpet.

Abruptly, I remembered the church we attended, which was on the other side of the school. On Sundays, we'd walk there with my mom. I saw a priest standing near the entrance and asked my mom if he was God. I also remembered asking if the nuns were devils, but I wouldn't get that answer until years later when I attended Catholic school.

I remembered my dad coaching football and allowing the students to play dodgeball, but that's where my memories of him stopped. It was strange I had no other memories of him.

Suzanne and I left the school; my memories guided our steps. I remembered the crosswalk guards holding little stop lights on a pole in the middle of the road. I remembered the dirt road that led to a grocery store and a field of cattails. We found what I thought may have been the old grocery store, but it was now a run-down storage unit and the dirt road had been paved.

I wondered whether something magical was in that blue paint that unveiled so many memories I never knew existed.

We later found the small apartment my family had shared, but I had to sheepishly admit my mom hadn't been neglectful in sending her little boy to walk the many miles uphill both ways to school. As it turned out, our apartment and the school were all within the distance of a football field. Things seemed so large and far away back then. Being a true friend, Suzanne didn't give me too much grief at my imagined childhood travails to trek to kindergarten.

Visiting the past with a crewmate is truly a bonding experience. However, creating new memories with a coworker can equally cement a relationship, especially if the circumstances are categorically awkward. We'd flown into the agricultural part of Mexico one afternoon and with some extra time before our return flight to the United States, Mike Finney and I were walking around to see the sights. Both of us were experienced international pilots who knew better than to eat tamales from a streetside cart. But you should have smelled those tamales. Each was individually wrapped in a corn husk; the spices wafted out, tantalizing our taste buds. The vendor, who spoke broken English, gave us full assurance that these would not cause us any problems.

Unfortunately, the American digestion system cannot compete with foreign street food.

At altitude, every bump of turbulence confirmed the folly of our decision. The tamales had been the perfect balance of corn meal, slow-cooked pork, and spicy green peppers; but now, those bastards were fighting a war against our intestinal tracts, which waged a losing battle for the wretched American pilots. Fortunately, we had to clear customs right as we crossed the Mexico-United States border. I can't recall much beyond the relief of the U.S. customs station restroom, but those tamales remain unforgettable.

Another bonding experience took place during my time at Vision Airlines with my friend, Tom Maier. We found ourselves entangled in a peculiar saga with the new Director of Inflight Services. It seemed the director had not familiarized herself with updated aviation practices since the 1950s; yet, was tasked with the crucial responsibility of training flight attendants to pass upcoming FAA check rides. Not surprisingly, she failed miserably, burdening me with the responsibility during an exceptionally busy period. A thorn in my side, she persisted in hindering our quest for airline certification. Fed up with her interference, especially during critical flight phases, I made a bold move. I gave an ultimatum to the company—it was either her, or me.

To my surprise, they shuffled her to a new position with a title so lengthy it escapes my memory. It seemed she was finally out of our hair, but I've been wrong before.

In her new role, she hatched an idea that bordered on absurdity. She allocated $15,000 to purchase crayons and coloring books to hand out to children on flights. Having two kids of my own, I voiced my concerns at the damage kids and crayons could cause to the interiors of new airplanes. No one listened. Instead, Tom and I were assigned the task of fetching the $15,000 worth of coloring books and crayons from the shipping company. Loaded into a rented van, the cargo became a heavy burden on our journey back to the office.

In a serendipitous twist, our route took us past an orphanage seeking donations. Tom and I seized the opportunity to redirect the destined crayons and coloring books to a more deserving cause. Every single item was handed over, and our fabricated excuse was that they were never delivered; we couldn't find them.

The bizarre episode of missing art supplies turned out to be the least of this airline's problems. It later surfaced that the company owners were involved in criminal activities, leading them to a fate behind bars. Amidst the chaos, Tom and I found solace in our small act of playing Robin Hood, turning a potential disaster into a colorful redemption.

Some people you just won't like, no matter how many shared experiences or long hours you're stuck together in a confined space. Some people are just assholes. A certain pilot I occasionally flew with was a real piece of work. I'll call him Dick to protect his true identity. He wasn't just unpopular with me, but with most of the pilots I knew. He was known as a tattletale. It was company policy that pilots were not allowed to loosen their neckties, even within the enclosed cockpit. This was a rule I disregarded often; and just as often, Dick reported me.

After my dislike for Dick had been cemented, we flew a private *Learjet* together. These machines are typically compact, built to maximize space on short flights for private clientele. This particular plane was equipped with what we called a "psychological potty", meaning the passengers knew it was there, but no one in their right mind would attempt to use it. In fact, it looks like any other seat on the airplane. The seat cushion lifts up and reveals a camper-type toilet underneath, devoid of any privacy.

The flight began normally enough until Dick

mentioned that his stomach hurt. I may have asked him if he'd eaten any tamales in Mexico, but I can't remember. Most likely I was too busy loosening my tie to pay much attention. It was a quick flight. We would barely hit altitude before we'd have to come back down for a landing. Dick let out a low moan beside me. A few minutes later he moaned louder. I noticed him clutching his stomach. Every few minutes, Dick's complaints grew more frequent. Maybe I tried to reassure him that we were landing soon, but not likely. I was probably just glad that he seemed too miserable to take any notes on my alleged misdeeds. Less than ten minutes out from landing, Dick bolted out of his flight chair and gave me full control of the airplane. He climbed out of the cockpit, rushing to the back and asked a woman to evacuate her seat. She'd been sitting on the psychological potty, strapped in with the seatbelt across her lap. The look of desperation on Dick's face must have been enough to send her scurrying. A moment later, Dick sank on the potty and relieved himself quickly and loudly while everyone looked away in horror. Even with their eyes closed, the smell permeated the small plane.

One passenger threw up, which caused another passenger to throw up. It was like a game of bodily function dominos, all while I was trying to land the plane.

I imagine it must have been some kind of nightmare for Dick, and no doubt the psychological potty did some serious psychological damage to everyone on board that day. I'd like to tell you about how much empathy I had for him, and how this horrendously mortifying situation turned into a shared story that forever bonded us. But the truth is he'd tattled on me too many times.

When the *Learjet* came to a stop, the door couldn't be opened quickly enough. The passengers bolted for the clean fresh air as though they were escaping a disaster zone. I guess, in a way, they were.

I'd also like to tell you that I usually keep that story to myself, in order to save Dick from embarrassment, and that I'm not the type of person to publish such a humiliating story about someone else in a memoir. But you know that's not true, because the proof is in your hands. I laugh every time.

Given the long hours and close proximity spent with co-workers, it's no wonder that I'm frequently asked about the rumored romantic lives between pilots and flight attendants. It's an excellent plot line for a movie or novel and one that worked better in the days before stereotypical gendered jobs became more inclusive. When I first started flying, it would have been virtually impossible for a flight attendant to get a pilot pregnant, but that's not the case anymore. In 1980, female pilots made up less than one-percent of the industry; while male flight attendants (often called stewards) represented less than five-percent. Today 20-percent of flight attendants are male, and fewer than ten-percent of pilots are female. The airline industry has a long way to go before someone says pilot and you don't automatically picture a white male.

That being said, it's true that pilots and flight attendants have affairs. It's also true that elementary teachers have affairs. Plumbers have affairs. Policemen, lawyers, doctors, United States Presidents, and dog trainers have affairs.

In the early days of my career, I worked for an airline that had a special wives' committee which installed rules to ensure that flight attendants never stayed in the same hotels as pilots. I don't know whether the wives on the committee understood that people could ride taxis or even walk between two hotels.

There are aspects of the airline world that fuel the romantic rumors between pilots and flight attendants. Up until the 1960s, it was a requirement that flight attendants be young, female, single, and meet certain physical standards. Many airlines even had frequent weigh-ins to ensure flight attendants maintained an attractive BMI. If a flight attendant got married or pregnant, or gained too much weight, she was out of a job.

Though marital status and gender requirements had relaxed by the 1980s when I came onto the scene, physical standards were still stringent, and weigh-ins were still mandatory. It was usually obvious when the weigh-in date was approaching because the stewardesses would often snap over simple requests; and women who were previously friendly, suddenly turned disagreeable. Starving people are not happy people. Once they'd been deemed acceptable by a number on a scale, they'd go back to their former cheerful demeanors, ready to smile and party again.

That being said, it was unusual to meet a flight attendant who wasn't exceptionally pretty. Meanwhile, it was perfectly acceptable for pilots to be overweight with big beer guts. By the 1990s, the airline industry began to embrace diversity and inclusion; and in recent years, has given focused attention to inclusive hiring practices.

Take a bunch of beautiful single women, fly them to remote locations with uniformed pilots, and you can understand the fuel behind the romantic rumors of the airline world. It's the perfect set up for a passionate fling. The term "'road wife'" was used occasionally for these mistresses, and I once had a guy tell me that he actually felt guilty going home to his wife, because he had fallen in love with his road wife.

It was impossible not to hear stories and talk once in a while. Several narratives definitely bounced around about wives showing up disguised as passengers in an attempt to catch husbands in betrayal. A few tales were shared in crew rooms about flight attendants involved in physical altercations on the plane before passengers loaded, due to love triangles gone awry. Fortunately, no crew tussles ever occurred on my flights. Before each flight, I liked to tell my crew, "This is a no drama flight. Should there be any drama, I'll ask you to step out onto the wing to handle it."

Again, inappropriate sexual liaisons are not unique to the airline world. But perhaps the physical appearance prerequisites of days gone by, the gender imbalance between pilots and flight attendants, as well my unarguably dashing facade in a uniform, have fed the rumor mill on this topic.

Funny things happen when you spend a lot of time with people. Working in such close quarters, you can't help but become friends. The jokes fall freely when you are out of hearing range of passengers.

On one occasion, our flight crew was walking through the terminal. We'd flown together all month and had shared many laughs. One of the flight attendants, an openly gay man, had become a friend. Right in front of us, a highly attractive woman wearing a low-cut dress bent over to pick up a child and we had to stop suddenly to avoid a collision. "Oh come on," I said to him, after we passed out of earshot. "I saw you staring at that woman as much as I was."

"Of course, I was staring," he told me. "But I was looking at her shoes."

Every so often, a co-worker's practical joke reached beyond the intended audience. I frequently worked as a check airman, a pilot who flies the requisite hours with brand-new pilots before they are released to the wolves. One day a fresh new pilot walked through my door, and I could immediately tell that she was sick with nerves. Part of a professional instructor's job is to encourage the student to relax. This day I was having no luck, but the last thing you want to do is go up in a plane with someone who is visibly so uncomfortable.

Finally, I asked her what was wrong, and I watched her blink furiously to stop the flow of tears. "Raymo told me you were a real asshole, and I was going to have a bad day with you."

Raymo was a good friend with a questionable sense of humor. This was his idea of a joke. I explained the situation to the frightened young woman and once the misunderstanding was cleared up, we had a very good training session.

An advantage of spending so many hours with fellow crew members is that you have a chance to rectify first impressions. The first time I met Danny Sprenger, he was a student whose reputation beat him to the cockpit. Though he was a very senior captain on smaller airplanes, he was brand new to a *Boeing*, so he had to go through me before he could fly passengers. Upon our first meeting, he introduced himself by telling me how senior he was, asked me where my tie was, and informed me that I needed a haircut. I'd dealt with hundreds of personalities over the years, but this one was certainly unique.

"Sir," I said, "if you think you're going to make it through this training we are going to have to talk about your attitude. The first thing you need to do is take off your tie and grow your hair longer."

Over the years we got to the point where we would just start laughing as soon as we saw each other, before even a word was spoken. Danny tells me he's a captain on the *747* now. I told him I'd have to see a picture before I'd believe it. I'm still waiting, Danny.

Tim Miles and I hit it off right from the start. He was a young guy with a bald head. I was an old guy with thick, black hair. The jokes started immediately. When Tim was offered a job with Southwest Airlines, I was working as a check pilot. I already knew that he was a good pilot. I already knew that he would have no trouble passing a normal simulator test. In fact, I'd made a plea to my boss to allow Tim to move into his grace period without the check ride, but FAA regulations said otherwise. So why not have a little fun and give Tim a test that he would not soon forget?

Two of the most difficult things you can give a pilot in the simulator is an engine failure on go-around or a slow leak, either fuel or hydraulic. The combination of an engine failure with a slow leak is such an unlikely occurrence in a real-life scenario that it would never be used in a normal check ride. But this wasn't going to be a normal check ride. Instructors will play with this scenario occasionally, mostly as a challenge. The outcome is usually not successful. The focus of the engine failure is so all-consuming, that the slow leak can escape notice, with severe consequences.

Tim wasn't surprised when I killed his engine. He handled it as well as could be expected. But I think his eye twitched a bit when he noticed the slow fuel leak, something that many pilots would have overlooked. I watched as his bald head turned a shade of red. He was flying with a single engine and transferring fuel. While Tim was in the midst of mitigating this disaster, I snuck in a hydraulic failure. He was now flying the simulator on manual reversion on a single engine.

Beads of sweat appeared on Tim's head. His muscles shook with exertion. I could tell he was pissed at me because this was beyond the scope of any normal procedure and served very little benefit outside of my own amusement. I was having fun back there, pressing any failure button that caught my attention.

Despite the near impossibility of the situation, Tim got that airplane on the ground successfully. He turned around to see me grinning in the instructor's seat. I could tell he was just about to rip into me, but I handed him his paperwork. "Nice ride."

"What was that?"

"To be honest," I told him. "I actually completed your paperwork last night before the check ride. That was just for fun."

Take that FAA.

As a kid, I never went to summer camp. There was no money for frivolities. Plus, my mom might've thought that summer camp sounded fun; and she had an unspoken rule that fun wasn't allowed with all the work to be done, real or imagined.

I have been fortunate to work in a field where fun and work have been combined, where I've made lifelong friends through shared experiences, and where every day feels like a new adventure waiting to be embraced.

19

Absence and the Heart

If a pilot's relationship with crew members is unique in the amount of time co-workers spend together on extended trips, a pilot's relationship with family members is equally unique in the amount of time spent away from each other on extended trips.

During my airline days, I remember a distinct conversation I had in the cockpit. I'd been lamenting to the co-pilot how often I'd been away from my family in recent months. As an offhand joke, and in reference to my jet-black hair that I'd inherited from my Mexican grandfather, he said, "You'd better be careful. Your next kid might come out with blonde hair and blue eyes."

I'm not going to lie. When my son Rob was born as blonde-haired and blue-eyed as his mother, I did a double take and inwardly questioned his DNA. His big sister Katie had been my clone at birth: thick dark hair, brown eyes, darker-toned skin. She still looks far more like me than Rob. There are times when I wonder how Rob could even be my son, but other times when I realize we are so alike he could only have come from me.

For the sake of my daughter, I should clarify that she looks like me only in the way that Mick Jagger's daughters or Steven Tyler's daughters resemble their fathers.

You can tell they are related; but in some unexplainable genetic happenstance, the daughters turned out gorgeous.

Katie and I have other similarities that extend beyond our striking good looks. We both left home at an early age. We were both born with independent spirits. We both had a clear view from youth about what we expected to do with our lives.

Comparatively, Rob and I have always lived in close proximity to each other. We've had the benefit of knowing we are just a stone's throw away if we need anything. We have even bonded over shared business ventures. Though I think the older I get, the more Rob contemplates moving farther away.

One of the great joys of fatherhood is when your children become your friends. It's a joyful transition moving from a parent-child relationship to friends. Now that my children are successful adults, I've on occasion asked them for advice. It's a strange turning of the tables and an incredibly fortunate stage of life where I'm privileged to receive sound counsel from the people I helped raise.

Pilots are not unique in traveling for work and spending long hours, days, or weeks away from family. Whole books have been written about the strain on families separated during long military deployments; while I don't mean to insinuate comparison to the sacrifices those men and women make, I do think there are a few commonalities between pilots, military personnel, pharmaceutical sales representatives, and other employees known for a heavy work travel schedule. We all worry about our kids while we are away, and we wonder what the consequences might be for all the time gone.

Funny enough, I've asked my kids a few times what they remember about me being gone constantly when they were little. Surprisingly, they've both said they have more memories of me being home all the time. One particular summer my daughter even asked me why I didn't have a job, since she was accustomed to all her friends' dads going to work each day. This was likely attributed to my months as a pool dad during a layoff.

Our childhoods shape our understanding of normal, and it may be that my children had a skewed impression of how often a dad was supposed to be around. My constant traveling had other ramifications on my children's perspectives. The first time Katie ever stayed overnight at a friend's house, she came home amazed at how big the soap bars and shampoo bottles were. "Did you know that towels come in colors other than white that don't have hotel names written on them?"

It's cliché to say that absence makes the heart grow fonder; honestly, I'd argue that no, it does not. As the absent family member, being gone does make you appreciate what you have at home, and you probably value the routine of home life more than the standard 9-5 employee. As the adult family member left behind, I think it makes you more resentful.

Single parenting is a hard role to play, but perhaps even more so for the person who doesn't single-parent regularly. Let me explain. For the parent who is single through widowhood, divorce, or by choice, there is an expectation they will be the person to establish the routine and rules, and they develop the mindset that they have to make a go of this alone. I'm not suggesting in any way that this is easy. But compare this to the sporadic single parent. This individual sets up routines, a system to make life work for the rest of the family while the spouse is gone, and then the spouse walks in and everything is disrupted. The established rules are broken. Things aren't done in exactly the same way.

From a business perspective, the best manager should be able to leave for a month unannounced, return, and find out that nobody realized he was gone. A long-standing pilot joke is that when you return home after being gone for two weeks and set your luggage at the door, your family looks up and says, "Are you going somewhere?"

But a family is not a business, nor is it a punchline in a joke.

I don't know whether I can blame fate or the alignment of the stars, but it did seem that whenever I left town, the worst things happened; and my wife, Beth, would be the one who was forced to pick up all the pieces by herself. Once when I was out of town, Rob was climbing a fence and sliced his arm open so badly that he still has a scar to this day. Just days after that, Katie received her diabetes diagnosis. I was at mandatory training. If I wasn't at the training, I would lose my job. It's a tough decision when you are forced between the choices of being there for your family or providing for them.

Whenever I was home, things seemed to operate smoothly, no credit to me. But when I left town, trees literally collapsed on our property, plumbing emergencies materialized, natural disasters of one sort or another descended upon Omaha. No doubt my time away felt even longer when combined with stressful life events that my wife navigated alone.

Surely, while the plagues descended upon my family in my absences, they imagined me in an exotic location somewhere, surrounded by gorgeous stewardesses in enchanting expensive restaurants on the beach in a tropical climate. In reality, I was most likely stuck in Newark in some crappy hotel in twenty degrees below zero weather with the wind howling and vibrating against the cheap windows as I struggled to microwave a burrito that I'd purchased from a vending machine, all while sitting on a questionable bedspread, still dressed in my uniform. At some point, I likely drifted off into a dream, the burrito soggy and forgotten, and in my hallucinatory state, there were absolutely gorgeous stewardesses on the beach, lovely restaurants, and exotic locations. I lived the dream until I heard pounding on my door and realized that Bertha from housekeeping was demanding I check out so she could clean my room.

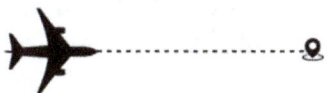

Friendships, like family, can be difficult to maintain when you are constantly traveling. At the end of a work trip, you come home to your family. Friendships take extra effort and scheduling.

I don't think there is an exact formula for lasting friendships, but I somehow got lucky in maintaining life-long relationships that began when I was very young. Two of my closest friends, Kenny Groves and Tom Ahrens, still live in Chadron, Nebraska. Another friend, Karla Hinman McConnell, also grew up with us in Chadron. Every second weekend in July, you can find the four of us, along with a good bunch of our high school classmates, back in Chadron where we celebrate Fur Trade Days. This small-town festival highlights the history of the French fur trading era, but the main reason to return home that weekend is to catch up with old friends.

The closer I get to retirement age, the more I appreciate the different types of friends I've gained along the way. My 'old' friends are people I've known for more than 50 years. These are the people who've walked through joy, fear, trauma, and sadness with me, and share memories of the tremendous amount of fun we've had together. The thing about an old friend is that you never have to tell him what's new, you just pick up where you left off. New friends are those I've known for more than ten years.

Acquaintances are people I've known for five or fewer years. And a work friend is someone I have worked with and wouldn't mind working with again.

Most people, regardless of their profession, battle the balancing act of work, family, and friends. Pilots, perhaps, gain the unique perspective that love doesn't know distance. Whether you are in the same town as your loved ones or 30,000 feet in the air, the most meaningful relationships have the flexibility to stretch out and stay connected.

20

Red Lights and Runways

It's been said that the biggest risk in life is the risk of doing nothing.

I don't usually think of my job as risky, given the number of safety precautions involved, but nothing in life is without risk. In the crisp air of January 2007, I found myself at the peak of my career, commanding the brand-new *Boeing 737-800* high above Midway Airport in Chicago. This busy airport, with its short runways, was a challenge on the best of days, but that day's horoscope gave a more ill-fated reading. It was the time of year when the nearby Lake Michigan likes to make ice, which is delightful for the local ice fishermen, but a trial for airports.

We were in a holding pattern, tracing our second circle through the sky, flying in what was previously reported as moderate icing. Mercifully, the new *Boeing* handled ice as well as anything I've ever known, but the collective groan from the passengers after I announced our delay was the least of my problems. The plane was close to minimum fuel.

The two planes in front of us had already declared minimum fuel to flight control, signaling that the people in the tower needed to expedite landing. Years of experience flying into Midway will teach you one thing. When the weather goes down, bring extra fuel. I once heard an old captain tell the kid running the fuel truck to pack the fuel in with a stick.

The first officer, an experienced and seasoned pilot, made eye contact with me. He knew what I knew. We'd be earning our money that day. Without being asked, he contacted the Midway approach. "Midway arrival Amtram 247, what is our sequence?"

"Amtram 247, number five."

We didn't say anything. While there was no need for immediate alarm, we'd now entered a position where there was no more room to screw around. The plane wobbled slightly as we hit patches of moderate turbulence, but this was also not a cause for concern. We heard through air traffic control that the fourth airliner in the holding pattern made the decision to abandon Midway and head to Chicago O'Hare, his alternate airport.

The two of us gave each other sideways glances. *Why did the pilot of number four think O'Hare was going to be any better?* But given that it moved us up one slot, we liked his decision. As more minutes went by, we took extra circles over the icy windy city below.

We were close to minimum fuel, but flight control had just cleared us for the approach. The surface wind picked up. The tower was now reporting some gusts. We were thirty to forty feet in the air when a bright red light illuminated the cockpit. To this point in my flying career, I'd never known a red light to be anything but bad.

The constant red glare of the cockpit light served as a scowling reminder as we descended closer to the ground at Midway. As captain, I decided to disregard the light and continue in for landing. Though the ice crystals bounced off our windshield, and I could almost feel the cold winter wind seeping through my uniform, the main wheels touched and the nose wheel came down gently. We had the auto brakes set to max, but once I knew they were working,

I released them and braked manually to give the passengers a smoother landing. As we arrived at the gate, my co-pilot and I shared deep breaths and smiles.

It was at that moment we remembered that the FAA had an agent in the jump seat doing a line check. We'd been very aware of his presence during the first part of the flight. After our initial conversation and introductions, it was strikingly apparent this individual was lacking in aviation experience, especially with big airplanes.

After, we noticed his skin had taken on a greenish tinge, and his knuckles were white and swollen from where he'd been gripping his seat cushion. A bead of sweat rolled past the front of his ear.

"I am going to have to go to my boss about this flight," he informed us.

I'd been to many FAA inquiries in my career, always as a union representative, but never as the intended lamb for slaughter.

The day of the inquiry arrived, and I took my seat at the table. We learned that the inspector's opinion was that when we saw the red light, we should have pulled up, circled around, and determined the cause of the light. What he didn't know was that the light was a feature put on new *Boeing*s to advise us of a blowup situation. Basically, it meant that during wind gusts, the flaps would release momentarily to avoid any damage. I'm not sure why they made the light red. It probably should've been green or orange.

My union rep stood up. "Do you mean to tell me we all gathered here today because you think the captain should've taken an ice-covered airplane with minimum fuel back into a holding pattern because a light came on telling him that everything was working properly?"

Years later I ran into the federal agent who'd handled the case. We spoke about that particular inquiry, and what became of the investigating agent who'd turned me in.

"You're not going to like our decision," he told me. "We decided to promote the inspector to a higher paying position with a fancier title."

I didn't mask my bewilderment.

"It's a desk job," the agent continued, "but it will keep him out of the airplane for the rest of his career."

I've been very fortunate to never encounter what I would consider a serious emergency on board an airplane. Experience is what told me I could land the airplane at Midway that day. What seemed risky to the inexperienced FAA agent was a perfectly managed situation.

Whether piloting a jet or pushing a baby stroller in the grocery store, you are managing risk. Risk is something that cannot be avoided, try as we might; but we can attempt to manage it. Deciding to take cover in bed all day because the world is too scary could be a risky decision. A tree could crash through the bedroom window; a meteorite could plummet through the roof; a fire could leave you trapped inside with no escape. Risk is an omnipresent threat, but pilots are equipped to keep a cool head in emergency situations.

When you are managing risk in aviation, you are doing nothing more than trying to increase the margin of safety. At 40,000 feet in the pressurized vessel of a modern airliner, you have fewer than seven seconds of useful consciousness should a depressurizing event occur. Were you paying attention to the flight attendant the last time you flew on a plane? Before each and every plane takes off, passengers are given instructions on what to do in the event of depressurization. How often do you get situated on an airplane and then take the time to count the number of seats between you and the nearest emergency exit? Did you even pay attention to where the closest emergency exit might be?

The level at which you choose to manage risk is a personal decision. I talk a lot about whether the shoes you choose to wear on the plane will help or hamper you if you are trying to exit a plane in a hurry. Other ways that passengers can manage their own risk on airplanes is to follow crew instructions, keep seatbelts fastened whenever seated, be mindful of personal items that could become dislodged in turbulence, know how to put the oxygen mask on correctly, and be aware of surroundings. You likely tuned that paragraph out just now, given how many times you've heard those instructions. But there's a reason they're repeated so often.

Safety is at the forefront of every pilot and crew member's mind. Passengers can play their part by taking personal responsibility to take safety regulations seriously.

Regulations pertaining to safety are in the books because somebody did something stupid. There are pages upon pages of regulations concerning the amount of fuel that must be carried. There are more pages of regulations pertaining to the amount of fuel that must be on the airplane when you land. We can assume these regulations are in place because someone flew an airplane without enough fuel on board.

Years ago, I was teaching the captain's Resource Management class. The purpose of the class was to improve communication, teamwork, decision-making, and situational awareness among flight crew members. One of the class participants was a man named Warren Pietsch. Warren is highly respected in the aviation community. He's flown everything in every facet of aviation. A founding board member of the Dakota Territory Air Museum and a famed warbird pilot, Pietsch can often be seen flying his famous *P-51C Thunderbird* at airshows.

On this particular day, the icebreaker on the syllabus was to name the best pilot you have ever known. Warren was generally the type of man who let his flying do the talking, so he sat quietly in the back. Whenever he did speak up, the room would get quiet, people would crank around in their seats so as not to miss a word. When it was his time to answer the question, I remember him saying without fanfare, "Well Don, that would probably be me. I'm the best pilot I've ever known."

My response was, "You're going to have to say more than that, Warren."

He continued. "I have been so hopelessly lost that I will never fly again without some preplanning. I have landed with such a low amount of fuel that I will always make sure I have extra. I have done a poor preflight and only discovered the issue in the air, and that will never happen again." He continued for several minutes, and of course the class silently soaked it in. I remember it so vividly because what he said was, "I have a lot of experience, and I use all of that experience every time I get close to an airplane."

Ron Howard directed the 1980 movie *Skyward* about a flight instructor at an old Texas airport teaching a paraplegic girl to fly. Bette Davis starred as the flight instructor, and the whole film was well-written, well-directed, and well-acted, at least until the last few minutes. During those last moments of the film, Ron Howard allowed the whole movie to be destroyed by things that would not have happened in the real aviation world. How much would it have cost to hire an aeronautics consultant to watch the movie? For God's sake, Ron, I would have done it as a favor to you for free.

I'm sure it's the same for policemen watching cop

shows, or lawyers watching courtroom dramas. The TV version of your career usually looks like a bunch of bullshit.

But in regard to the *Skyward* movie, I know most people who watched it didn't catch it. Ron Howard probably didn't care. The actors didn't know any better. But in reality, had the situation proceeded like the movie suggested, it would have ended in certain death for the new student on her first solo and for several innocent bystanders on the ground. Furthermore, Bette Davis's character would have been convicted in civil court and had her pilot's license removed.

In real life, safety is the primary concern for every flight. Safety is safeguarded through extensive pilot training and checklists, equipment redundancy, and experienced pilots. Risks can be mitigated by taking personal responsibility and by taking the time to prepare for possible emergency situations.

Risks cannot be eliminated, only managed. So, if you are thinking of staying in bed all day to avoid danger, at least make sure you are in an underground bunker with fire-safe walls, sealed off from all outside contaminants. You should probably also wear a tinfoil hat.

21

Wings of Progress

My grandmother, Olevia Delsing Lliteras, was born in 1900. At the time of her birth, the Wright Brothers were already working on their famous airplane, but their first successful flight was still three years in the future. Commercial air travel was another fourteen years coming. The year my grandmother was born, only 8,000 automobiles existed in the whole country; and they were likely not evenly distributed into western Nebraska, where my grandma was a resident.

Grandma Olevia was a woman of the new century. She was a hard-working devout Catholic, raised eight children, countless chickens, and sometimes on weekends she went dancing with my Grandpa John. John (Juan) Lliteras was a mean son of a bitch, but when he got after me for doing dumb kid things, Grandma would stick up for me. She was a collector of S&H Green Stamps, and when her book was full, she mailed it in for a brand-new guitar to replace the mouse-infested broken instrument that I'd salvaged from the dump. Always the entrepreneur, I gathered pop bottles to sell back to the bottle redemption centers. Grandma would drive me the 42 miles between Chadron and Hemingford, because the Piggly Wiggly in Hemingford would pay me three cents for each pop bottle, rather than the measly two cents I got in Chadron.

It was during one of those drives that I asked her the question that was at the forefront of my eight-year-old mind. "Grandma, do you believe in time travel?"

"Of course I believe in time travel!"

"Really? Wow!"

"If someone had told me when I was your age, that someday I could get on a machine that would fly me from one side of the country to the other, I never would have believed it," she said. "At the time, flight seemed just about as absurd as time travel."

She went on to tell me about the first time she ever rode in a train as a little girl. The train reached a top speed of around 32 miles per hour. For Grandma, and for most of the other passengers on the train, this was the fastest speed they'd ever traveled. Before that train ride, most people had only experienced speed on the back of a horse. She remembered passengers praying, panicking, some suggesting that maybe they should jump off. Olevia just looked out the window and wished the train would go even faster.

In the beginning days of train travel accidents were fairly common, resulting in significant loss of life and injuries. Safety regulations struggled to keep up with the expanding infrastructure. Limited communication and human error led to sometimes deadly mistakes.

Today travelers hop on automated trains devoid of human drivers without a second thought. Automated controlled systems, sensors and cameras, collision avoidance and communication systems, emergency stop buttons, redundancy and fail-safe systems, as well as cybersecurity measures all make train travel safe and easy.

Early model automobiles were considered death traps by some. Cars lacked basic safety features, had ineffective brakes and less predictable handling; not to mention, road conditions were often abysmal and lacked proper signage, lighting, and standardized markings. A lot of people died attempting to use a match to check fuel levels because they didn't have a basic understanding of gasoline. Over the years, that problem has been solved with technology and possibly some self-correcting of the gene pool. In modern America, getting a license to drive a car at age 16 is simply a rite of passage; and while parents usually experience increased anxiety at this milestone, cars are considered a safe and reliable mode of transportation.

Airplanes were certainly not regarded as safe in the early days. Cloud sailing was deemed an appropriate pastime only for the birds and daredevils. Crowds would gather to watch aeronautic acrobats, not only with amazement, but also with morbid voyeurism. Like my grandmother, most people in the early 1900s could not imagine a time when air travel would be considered a normal part of life.

There's always risk as new technologies are adapted. Even Socrates, a fifth-century Greek philosopher, expressed concern with written words, which were a departure from traditional oral teachings, because he worried the words would reach people who didn't have the understanding for interpretation. It's not hard to assume what Socrates might have said about the Internet.

The newest scary bogeyman of the future is Artificial Intelligence. But you don't need a time-travel machine because AI is already weaved into many facets of our daily lives, including in the cockpit. Almost every feature of modern-day jets is assisted with some sort of AI. From flight management systems, automated takeoff and landing systems, collision avoidance, to weather prediction, AI has become an integral tool in modern aviation. Pilots undergo extensive training to operate and manage these systems correctly. But will a day come when pilots aren't needed at all?

Some people are nervous about allowing a computer to 'think' and make decisions. But I can see a tremendous value in having a tool that is capable of making quicker and more accurate decisions, especially in times of emergency, without being subject to human emotions. In the future, I can very easily see more cars without drivers and planes without pilots. Driverless cars have already been tested, and while the public has not been convinced as of yet, I think given time we will see a day when we don't think twice about hopping in autonomous vehicles. Airplanes will be next.

When I was teaching my kids to drive, I felt pretty confident in their ability behind the wheel. It was all the other drivers on the road that made me worry. Without humans in the driver's seat, we lose the stress of distracted drivers answering texts, reaching into the backseat to console the crying baby, or just not seeing the car in the other lane. AI offers the ability to increase the margin of safety and limit risk.

It's my belief that AI will stand the airline industry on its head. The learning curve of AI in the cockpit will be steep. At first, there could be tragedies; but eventually, we'll stop checking the gasoline gauge with matches and the kinks will get ironed out.

Adapting to new technology can be a challenge. In the mid-1980s, I worked for Braniff 2. The airline considered purchasing a fleet of the newly released *Airbuses*, rumored to be the next big thing in cutting-edge technology. Everyone was eager to fly them, but only the most senior pilots were sent for training. Upon returning, they were discouraged and defeated. They'd failed the course. They told horror stories of things like fuel computers, Fly-by-Wire (FBW), and side stick control. In reality, they were just resisting change. They liked doing things the old way and felt comfortable flying the old airplanes.

Those senior pilots have my sympathy. I grew up driving a manual car. The first time I ever drove with an automatic transmission was during a summer driver's training course. I had as much experience as you could possibly have as a 17-year-old who started driving long before it was legal. At that point in my life, it already felt like second nature to sit behind the steering wheel. But the power steering on an automatic transmission was new and different. I remember thinking, Huh, this is cool, but ultimately decided I'd rather stick with the old stuff I already knew.

For the record, today my car is so automatic it keeps me from drifting across the center line or coming too close to an object while backing up. I've gotten used to these safety features and even miss them when I'm in a rental car that doesn't have the same systems.

Unfortunately, Braniff 2 bit the dust before I ever had a chance to fly those new *Airbuses*, but I would have loved the opportunity. As aviation continued to move forward in technology, I soon got my chance at automation. My first automated flight was in a *Boeing 737NG*. At first it was challenging, but once I got a feel for it, I hated the thought of having to return to an old steam gauge airplane. The automation in the *Boeing 737NG* relieved the workload in the pilot's seat and increased spatial awareness. The machine was designed to fly at the highest level of automation, and even check rides were flown with the autopilot on. The plane was managed rather than flown.

I'm a firm believer in supporting new and advancing technologies in aviation. Accident reports are often traced to a pilot being overloaded or overwhelmed in an emergency situation. With mere seconds to make the right decisions, quick thinking is paramount. Legendary American football coach Vince Lombardi once said, "We didn't lose the game, we just ran out of time." In an emergency situation, time becomes the most precious commodity. As AI becomes more ingrained in aviation, I propose simple questions. *Can the machine think better than I can? Can it think faster than I can?* I believe the answer is yes.

There will always be those who resist technology. My mom believed cell phones were stupid and overly consuming, and she left this world without ever owning one. Perhaps her life was better for it, but I enjoy keeping track of my friends on Facebook and having the ability to navigate to a new restaurant in an unfamiliar town with the touch of a button.

Politicians and insurance companies will likely be the biggest holdouts in the progression of technology in aeronautics, but as the pilot, mechanic, and general labor shortages increase daily, AI is a logical choice.

With proper implementation and training, AI will be the next step in aviation modernization. Current equipment is maintained and replaced on a timed schedule, rather than when it's actually broken. AI could save the airline money and passengers' lives by being able to accurately forecast equipment failures. AI could also be used to monitor every system on every airplane in between inspections, catching problems in real-time for immediate reporting allowing quick action to be taken. A similar system could also be used to monitor the pilot's health or even mental capacity at any given moment. At present, planes require at least two pilots, for obvious reasons. If one pilot has a heart attack or other health calamity, the plane must have a backup. AI could potentially make single-piloted aircraft a safe option. However, this personal information would need to be guarded and kept out of the hands of the government, which you and I know is likely a foregone conclusion. I would be very uncomfortable knowing that anyone besides myself had access to such sensitive information.

As you can see, I fear human intervention and greedy human nature far more than I fear Artificial Intelligence.

It'll be hundreds of years before we can get a machine to care as much about my ass in that cockpit seat as I do; but in the meantime, advancing technology is the way forward for safer transportation. Aviation has always been on the foremost edge of technology. In the interest of safety, I hope that remains true.

I'm excited for the time machine to be invented. The first place I'll go is back to the highway between Chadron and Hemingford and tell Grandma Olevia all about it.

22

Confidence in the Cockpit

If you asked someone which careers attracted the biggest egos, I'd be willing to place a bet they'd respond with surgeons, lawyers, CEOs, politicians, and pilots. The bigger the responsibility, the bigger the ego. I'm not sure whether the chicken or egg came first, and it's hard to say if the jobs created the egos, or if the egos convinced people that they would do these jobs. I'll be the first to admit that I've met considerate, kind, and humble people who represent each of these career fields–even politicians. However, stereotypes exist for a reason.

I imagine that you'd have to have a high self-esteem to stand over a patient with a knife in your hand and think, *I'm going to cut into this human and save his life.* When you have power over others and responsibility for their well-being, you need confidence in your training and your ability to do the job well.

As a patient, I'd prefer the surgeon with a confident, steady hand, who can assure me they know exactly what they are doing rather than the super humble one who says they're not so sure this is going to work.

I once told a friend that my hands are responsible for more lives than a surgeon's. He gave me a sideways glance and said, "With that philosophy, I guess a bus driver could say the same thing." Point taken. He was absolutely correct.

Appearances can be deceiving. I've read enough articles and books about famous actors, musicians, and comedians to know that no matter what is presented on the surface, everyone deals with self-doubts and inner demons. Perception tells us that some professions are filled with big egos, but everyone faces doubt and fear. It's what makes us human. I still question whether politicians are human, but this is supposed to be a book about pilots.

Mark Ramsey, a friend and fellow pilot, used to do a routine as passengers lumbered onto the plane. He'd stand in the galley in full uniform with the bathroom door propped open. In a voice just loud enough for an occasional passenger to hear, he'd look in the mirror and deliver self-affirmations, "Mark, you are a highly trained professional. You can do this. You are a good person and people will like you. You will soon be in command of a very sophisticated machine, and you will perform admirably."

It never got old. It was funny every time.

Though Mark was intentionally performing comedy, I would be amazed to hear of a pilot sitting in the cockpit, ready to fire up the engines, who had never had doubt fill his mind. The doubt may be as simple as wondering whether the forecast would clear or as complex as knowing if the plane goes down, pilot error will likely be to blame. Whatever confidence or egotism a pilot may exude, at the end of the day, they carry a huge responsibility for a lot of people, and better not mess up.

Fortunately, pilots have a great deal of assurance in their abilities, which doesn't hurt. Egotism and self-confidence are sometimes difficult to distinguish.

As technology becomes more sophisticated, however, humans become the weak link in a system. Humans don't have a switch to compartmentalize our brains to think only of aviation when we're at the controls. We can't push a button to clear brain fog for the few seconds it takes your mind to categorize a problem and find the corrective action. Unlike when you are training with a simulator, there is no reset button to clear the problem and set you back at the end of the runway.

On dark nights in the cockpit, I often gaze out the window. There, mirrored on the opaque glass, I can usually see my own reflection. And for the most part, that's the only person you can really count on during an emergency. Of course, flying a big airliner is a team operation, and hopefully you are right to put your trust in all the other team members who worked to get that plane in the sky. But humans do make mistakes, and at the end of the day, you are bearing the brunt of the responsibility.

What's the difference between an air traffic controller's mistake, a mechanic's mistake, and a pilot's mistake? If the pilot makes a mistake, the pilot dies. If the air controller makes a mistake, the pilot dies. If the mechanic makes a mistake, the pilot dies.

Pilots must work hard to combat human error, self-doubt, and even over-confidence. I have found a few strategies in my life that seem to work in every situation. The top three are communication, communication, and of course, communication. As a pilot, it's my responsibility to act as a leader to the crew. I've found the more you can communicate with others, the more likely your team will fuse together and eliminate mistakes. As a leader, if I can empower the first officer, the flight attendants, even the gate agents and mechanics, then I have a whole team of people who are working to make our company look good and to take every measure to provide a safe and comfortable flight. This is a skill that translates well beyond the cockpit. Enabling those around you to be at their best will usually have the added benefit of making you look good, too.

23

It's a Small World

More than 331 million people live in the United States. It's estimated that 110,000 of those American residents are airline pilots. With these numbers, your chance of crossing paths with a pilot is about 1 in 3000.

When my son was a very young boy, someone asked him if he was going to be a pilot when he got big, just like his daddy. I remember his response. "No, everybody's a pilot."

In his world it was true, but he had a skewed perspective, limited by the narrow scope of childhood, where pilots seemed as common as any other profession.

With such a relatively miniscule number of pilots, compared to the United States population, it's no wonder that the aviation world is a small one.

In the early 1950s, commercial air travel experienced a surge, and airlines around the world began expanding their fleets to offer more connections and destinations for travelers. I imagine as people traveled greater distances than ever before, the concept of a small world came into focus. All of a sudden, journeys that took months or even years, could be accomplished in days.

I have often gazed down on the shadow of the airplane flitting across the wheat fields and cattle pastures of the Great Plains, and I find myself imagining what it must have been like to walk across this country as one of the pioneers in a wagon train. When the Mormons left their winter headquarters here in Omaha, they traveled less than two and a half miles on the first day. There is a historical marker close to what is now the North Omaha Airport that reads, "the first campsite of the Mormons after leaving their winter quarters." The world must have felt large indeed if a journey less than a 5K was momentous enough for a plaque.

I am thankful the world is so small today that I could visit both my children in the same week and still attend the latest John Fogerty concert.

Airplanes have made the world seem physically smaller. Travel destinations that were once just impossible hearsay can now be experienced by anyone who has the money to pay for a ticket. However, it's the interconnectedness of human relationships that makes the world seem especially tiny to me.

In London, I once walked into a pub and sat down next to Steve Staples, a fellow pilot I'd flown with years ago. I greeted him, and he casually turned around and said, "Hi, Don." While this type of story always amazes my non-pilot friends, it never feels like a big deal to those of us in the industry. A lot of airlines use the same hotels, and a lot of pilots have worked for many airlines. So, although having an impromptu dinner with a friend halfway across the world isn't remarkable, it's a pleasure that never gets old.

The small world of aviation can either work for or against you. A benefit is that you likely know somebody somewhere who can answer your question, locate a plane part, or offer you a job. I've built many bridges in my career, and I honestly feel I could go back to anyone I've worked for in the past, and they would welcome me with open arms. From a hiring perspective, it's a tremendous advantage to look at someone's resume and know the individuals on their reference sheet.

I still serve as a reference for pilots today. Proper etiquette says that if you use someone's name for a reference, you'd better clear it with them first. People know that I will be 100-percent honest should someone call me for a recommendation. Fortunately, 99-percent of the people I know would receive a glowing recommendation from me.

For less respected pilots, the small world aspect of aviation can be detrimental. There are good pilots who are bad employees, and good employees who are bad pilots. There are pilots who are average at both; and of course, great ones who excel at both. In such a close-knit community, you can't hide your reputation easily. I've been advised by many wise pilots to always be careful of who you piss on in this business. That urine-soaked individual could very likely be your next boss. I've seen that exact scenario play out many times.

After American Trans-Air went out of business, I was hired in a management position with Vision Airlines. It was a great pleasure to call up my old friends and offer them jobs. During that time, jobs were scarce and many of my friends were left empty-handed when ATA shut down. Unfortunately, Vision Airlines also went out of business shortly after, due to dishonest owners. This is not an exaggeration; a couple of them went to jail. But I did enjoy feeling a bit like Santa Claus while it lasted.

I have two teenage nieces who, upon learning I was writing a book about pilots, said they'd probably only read it if it had something to do with Taylor Swift. Having not met her personally, and not considering myself a fan of her music, I wasn't sure how I'd be able to fit that in. But it just so happens that in this small world of aviation, I've attended several training courses with Taylor Swift's pilots.

I remember faces and I remember the stories

people have told me. Most of the time I remember what kind of car they drove and where they lived. But some of their names have eluded me over the years. One of the most enjoyable things about being in a small world is how quickly you pick up from where you left off with old friends, whether or not you remember their names. It could have been years since we'd talked, or maybe we only flew together a couple of times, but we are quick to reestablish these fast friendships and continue to build on it until the next time.

One of my favorite places to connect with old friends is the Experimental Aircraft Association (EAA) AirVenture Oshkosh, which takes place at the Wittman Regional Airport in Oshkosh, Wisconsin. As one of the largest, world-renowned aviation events, this annual gathering attracts aviation enthusiasts, pilots, and aircraft from every corner of the planet. It's fun to watch the myriad of airshows, take in the vintage and military aircraft demonstrations, exchange ideas with others in the business, and celebrate flight. Unlike Disney World, Oshkosh actually is the happiest place on Earth for pilots. You can't walk ten feet without bumping into someone you know.

Attending the EAA each year is like a high school reunion, only better because no one remembers your awkward haircut from sophomore year. Tens of thousands gather, and many choose to camp on the grounds during the event, adding to the festival-like atmosphere. It's a family-friendly event, and many pilots bring their children, introducing the next generation to the joy of flying. The EAA's Young Eagles program provides free introductory flights to young attendees. Older participants can attend workshops and seminars, or just enjoy the spectacular aerial shows.

Each year a man who calls himself "The Preacher" shows up with an insulated coffin that he keeps stocked with beer. Those in the know can gather round, take a beer, and enjoy companionship. The rule is if you take a beer, you leave a beer, so there's always a diverse variety of choices.

It's often said if you get a group of men pilots together with their wives, all they want to talk about is airplanes. If you get a group of men pilots together without their wives, all they want to talk about is women. This year in Oshkosh, I took a break under the shade of an awning and enjoyed a bottle of iced water from one of the coolers. I realized that the awning belonged to a women's pilot organization. From a distance, I could hear the women's voices, but I couldn't make out what they were saying. I wish I could have gotten closer to hear what exactly it is that women pilots talk about. I guess I'll never know.

Pilots are an opinionated bunch. I once heard that if you stood ten pilots in front of the atomic clock, you would get ten opinions of what time it is. But despite our differences, we are unified in our love for flight, our bond of working in an often incomprehensible industry, and our close-knit community that forms the small world of aviation.

24

The Legacy of Flight

The first time my son, Rob, took our *Grumman American AA-5 Cheetah* down the Blair Municipal Airport runway by himself, I didn't take my eyes away from the plane. I carefully and thankfully noted that the windsock hung limp, the Nebraska sky was clear, and the only clouds were distant cirrus wisps. I steadied my cell phone to video the experience, and hoped against hope that I'd taught him everything he needed to know in case something went wrong.

Though I'd been a flight instructor for nearly all of my aviation career, it had been years since I'd taught a primary student. And as I stood in the still air, watching the plane gather speed, I realized I'd never before soloed someone I loved.

Rob surprised me when he initially told me he wanted to learn to fly. He'd never shown much of an interest in flying, beyond his love of travel, and his pursuit of aviation brought back a new level of fun into flying. With his characteristically wry sense of humor, Rob told me, "Well Dad, someday you are going to be dead, and I'm going to have to pay someone else to teach me. So, we'd better do it now."

Together, we purchased the *Grumman Cheetah*, a single-engine, low-wing monoplane with fixed landing gear. It was in excellent condition; the previous owner, Gary Hausmann, took impeccable care of it. I wanted Rob to learn on an older airplane because flying old steam gauges will do nothing but enhance a student's ability if he ever decides to fly the new equipment. Older planes also have the ability to teach a hands-on-feel that the newer planes lack.

Many schools of thought exist on how to teach a new flight student. The most common method involves teaching maneuvers visually and then immediately transitioning to instrument-based training. This approach is efficient and enables students to progress through the syllabus rapidly; but if there's a weakness in modern-day students, it's their inability to just look out of the window and fly the plane.

Since Rob doesn't have to pay for a flight instructor and we own the airplane, I've decided to teach him the visual art of flying first. We'll save instrument work for a later time. In fairness to the modern student, the prevalent use of advanced automation systems and the busy air traffic control environment make visual flying less pertinent. Additionally, modern flyers may never be required to develop the hands-on-feel of flying a plane, which was once considered fundamental.

During one of our flight sessions, while Rob was flying parallel to the runway (a phase known as downwind while preparing to land), I simulated an engine failure—a common training scenario. What made this incident unusual was Rob's calm demeanor, excellent hand-eye coordination, and his ability to glide the airplane to the end of the runway without engine power. I couldn't have been prouder, and his newfound self-confidence was palpable.

I've insisted that Rob be present for the annual inspections of the aircraft and observe as much maintenance as possible when his schedule allows. We call this chair flying, or hangar flying. A vast amount of knowledge can be learned simply by understanding how the plane works, talking about flying, or even watching other pilots fly.

Having grown up without the guidance of a father figure, I became a dad without a legacy to pass on. Our family didn't have a lot of traditions, other than working hard and making sure there was enough money to cover the monthly needs, not wants. I used to be jealous of all my friends who went hunting with their dads on weekends, so much so that I saved up my money, went down to Western Auto and bought my own .410 shotgun and shells. I walked through town, clutching my new shotgun, determined to take myself hunting. I remember standing alone out in a field on the outskirts of town. I fumbled with the chamber, shoving the shells inside, unsure exactly how to tell whether it was properly loaded. Raising the gun, I haphazardly shot at a bevy of pheasants about 30 yards away and only succeeded in scaring them. As I watched the last few birds take to the sky, I thought about how all the other kids had it made. They had dads to teach them how to do this. Perhaps to compensate for my lack of a father, I changed the narrative in my head. Instead of feeling jealous of my friends, I chose to feel superior. They didn't have the skills to figure things out for themselves. If their dads were busy with work, or out on a drunken bender, my friends had to wait around for their old men to come around. I decided I was pretty lucky that I didn't have to rely on someone who didn't have the time to teach me things. My dad wasn't coming around, so I taught myself.

Flying with Rob, it came to my attention that while I didn't inherit a legacy from my own father, I created my own. Teaching Rob to fly and imagining that he may someday teach his own children to fly, is a legacy I'm proud to share with future generations.

Flying has deepened the friendship I share with my

son. He's surpassed me in most areas of knowledge at this point, but flying is still a sector where I know something he doesn't. He can't help but respect his old man up in the sky, because his life depends on it.

Sometimes I think about the could've-beens and should've-beens with my own father. I don't have a friendship with him. I don't have respect for him. He showed up in Omaha years ago when Katie and Rob were little, and he came out to see me and to meet them. Katie and I had invented a game on the trampoline. I'd throw footballs to her and she'd soar up into the sky to catch them. My dad stood watching. Having been a football coach his whole life, he stopped me mid-toss. "Here, Donald, let me show you a better way to throw."

How dare that son of a bitch try to teach me how to throw a football! There I was, 42 years-old, and my dad was trying to coach me. I wanted to ask him, *where the hell were you when I really wanted someone to teach me how to throw a ball?* But I held my tongue. There's no point in fighting with someone when you have no interest in making up.

That night, I lay in bed, just as pissed off as I could be. I thought of all the students and athletes my dad must have taught over his career, and how those virtual strangers inherited more of a legacy from that man than I ever would. But then I thought of my own children, asleep in their beds just down the hall from mine. They'd never have to stand out in a field alone trying to figure out how to shoot a gun or toss a ball, because they knew that I'd always be there to teach them whatever they wanted to know.

Being present in my children's lives is perhaps the greatest legacy I could ever hope to pass on.

The newer *Boeing* aircraft have the *NG* designation behind the number, for instance, the *Boeing 737NG*. The *NG* stands for next generation.

Back when I regularly worked as a flight instructor, I'd often ask myself how to teach this next generation of pilots. I was beginning to notice a few disturbing commonalities shared between *NG* pilots: a lack of respect for older aviators, a sense of entitlement, a less-than-acceptable work ethic, a disregard for punctuality, and above all a lack of patience.

My generation is not unique in worrying about what the young are going to do with the world we've built. Thankfully, the new generation of students inspires me as much as it concerns me. I've discovered many remarkable traits amongst them: high intelligence, ability to comprehend information with surprising quickness, access to learning tools, and the ability to use them flawlessly. New technology in no way intimidates today's students.

I can easily remember feeling lost as a brand-new pilot and feeling the need to hide behind a veneer of know-how, acting with the confidence of an astronaut just returning from my latest shuttle mission. Today's students seem to require more babysitting, therapy in the flightdeck, and occasional pats on the shoulder. In the big picture, I'm not sure that my lifelong technique of emotional suppression was any better than just being honest with my feelings and admitting that, at times, I was nervous, lacked confidence, and wondered what I was doing in a plane, dressed up like a pilot.

I remember a particular student who was exceedingly nervous, which never bodes well for a training session. Some instructors like to drill students with oral questions while they are preparing for pushback and take-off, though that was never my personal style. In this situation, however, I needed to break the tension. As he made his preparations, I asked him to give me the memory items for inadvertent deployment of the thrust reverser on take-off. Anyone in his position would know those basic commands, and he began to spew them out.

I stopped him. "No, no, no."

He froze, confused and unsure of what to do next.

"According to the FAA, you've got to blame some-one for the problem before you do anything else. Now, most of the time it'll be the FAA's fault, but they prefer you find someone else to point a finger at. So, who do you want to condemn to make the government happy in this go-round?"

He laughed and the tension was released.

Other students need tense situations to demon-strate their capabilities. A student I will always remember is Eddie Hernandez. He was probably one of the best stu-dents I ever instructed. He was probably also the youngest captain I ever taught, only in his late 20s, I would guess, but looked more like he was 12. One day we were doing three separate observation rides, meaning three new cap-tains would complete their final phase of training, which was to ride with the FAA. The middle flight would be the trickiest and most stressful flight of the day because it was a positioning flight. On this quick, seven-minute flight the pilot would be required to complete all the tasks that would usually be demonstrated on a longer flight. The three flyers were two experienced captains and Eddie.

"I'm going to put you on the short positioning flight," I told Eddie. "Do you know why I'm giving you this leg?"

"Yes sir," he said. "Because the old experienced guys

probably can't handle it, and I obviously don't know what I'm getting into."

I said, "You are correct."

Although it was only a seven-minute flight, it was one of the best executed check rides I have seen. Eddie is a captain for United Airlines today.

Every student learns differently, and grasps concepts at different times. I have always felt that a good instructor can teach a student what they need to know, but a great instructor can think of three separate ways to explain the same thing until a light comes on in the student's eyes.

My daughter, Katie, has been rebuilding an old farmhouse in Tennessee, which has been a completely new level of learning for her. She has become well-versed at wiring, plumbing, drywalling, paneling, fence building, and tile work. She asked me whether I was more impressed by her being a doctor, or for her ability to wire a 220-volt circuit, or install a three-way switch. I told her I know a lot more doctors than people who could wire a three-way switch from memory. Katie has gained most of these skills from watching YouTube videos.

Most of what I've learned about home remodeling has been the result of shocks, cuts, burns, or other injuries. I imagine that if I'd pursued home remodeling as a career and attended an accredited school with a strict syllabus, I would have learned a lot of what I learned from the school of hard knocks. At the end of the day, my project would likely have been just as safe and secure; but had I followed the syllabus, I wouldn't have been able to describe in vivid detail what it feels like to be shocked by a 110-volt current because of a wire I forgot I was holding in my hand while trying to connect another wire to an outlet.

The instructors whom I've admired the most are the ones who can recognize different learning styles and play to the student's strengths, whether that means giving them the full play-by-play before entering the airplane or allow-ing them to learn from their mistakes.

It has been one of my greatest aviation privileges to be in a position to teach the next generation of pilots. Amazingly, I've learned far more from attempting to teach another person than I could ever have imagined learning as a student. Embracing the challenges of guiding the next generation, I've discovered that in teaching, we don't just impart knowledge; we continually learn, evolve, and find profound meaning in the shared journey of flight.

25

The Call of the Clouds

I've imagined what it must feel like to perform on a stage, entertaining an audience of thousands. What pressure must you feel, knowing that each audience member paid hard-earned money to spend a few hours watching you perfectly execute your skills? Beyond the pressure, I would hope that you would feel immense privilege knowing you've been given an opportunity to do something very few people have ever had the chance to do.

As a professional pilot, I've been offered a glimpse of what goes through a performer's mind. The flight deck, while not as prominent as a stage, is an exclusive seat reserved for only 0.004-percent of the population. This restricted chair is where airline pilots fly the public into the stratosphere, where they've been trusted by people paying hundreds of dollars believing they will perform their skills at the highest level, safely and effectively.

Aviation is a very small world. While we may look like a diverse group of people, we are unified by an internal conviction knowing we had the privilege to answer the call of the clouds. We felt the pull of the sky and took mankind to places where, without human innovation and technology, survival would never have been possible.

Pilots persevere. In a career plagued with layoffs and financial insecurity, pilots persist in chasing contrails across the sky. We are a group who overcame the economic downturns of the 1980s, the devastation of 9/11, social roadblocks that prevented comfortable retirements, and the financial fallout of the Covid-19 Pandemic. There were many times in the course of the more than 20,000 hours that I've logged in a plane that I wondered if I should just take a job as a banker. But never in those 20,000 hours did I imagine I would ever stop flying. Each time I feel the thrust of an airplane taking off and rising above the troubles on the ground, I'm returned to a place where I've known I belonged since childhood.

George Bernard Shaw said, "Youth is wasted on the young." But I wonder, is wisdom wasted on the old? I used to tell my daughter to never confuse knowledge, education, and wisdom. They are three distinct disciplines, and one doesn't necessarily help you acquire the next. It seems when we get to our highest level of wisdom, our bodies and brains begin to break down, and we are quickly surpassed by the younger generations as they make their own mistakes, fail, and try again, all in the pursuit of turning their knowledge and education into wisdom.

Having worked as a flight instructor for most of my career, one of my greatest accomplishments has been to see a lightbulb come on for a student and watch them perform a feat which felt like an impossibility the day before. That's the goal and the reward. But to see a student surpass you in knowledge and ability is an honor that has been one of my greatest privileges. Perhaps even more astounding is hearing yourself ask your child for advice. While some might see this as slipping or weakness, I think of it as the ultimate achievement.

At the risk of sounding philosophical, I feel a touch of immortality knowing that I've passed on something that will outlive me. The thought that someday my former students will teach new students, or that my son may teach my grandson or granddaughter to fly, is a greater fulfill-ment than I could ever get from a stage in front of thou-sands of people.

Many years ago, when the airplanes were open cockpits, and the best pilots were the brave ones, and the bold pilots were no longer with us, piloting was a young man's game. When health issues intervened, or mental faculties dulled, it was time for the old pilots to hang up their goggles.

There are two things in aviation that I've always hated: firing someone, and telling someone their perfor-mance was no longer up to the minimum standards that allowed them to continue in the training program. If some-one was fired, they deserved it, but I still felt bad. But what really pulled at my heart was when an older gentleman, who had maybe six months to go before retirement, did not perform well enough in the simulator to continue. At that point, the union would protect his pay for the next six months, and early retirement would begin.

You would see some guys, so desperate to stay in the sky that they would try again and fail a second or third time. At that point, the union would no longer pay for early retirement. Instead, the pilots were forced out, no longer able to hang their goggles with dignity.

Early on I decided when I'm ready to hang up the goggles, it will be completely my choice. Not the doctor's decision, or the chief flight instructor's pronouncement, or the people I work for, or my friends and family – selfish as it may sound, I want that decision to be mine and only mine.

Today I'm enjoying this stage of semi-retirement, where flying now feels like a well-paid hobby and I still have time to play music with a local band, keep up with my rental properties, and soak in the hot tub. I feel incredibly blessed to live the life I have lived for more than 50 years. Though as much as I've enjoyed almost every facet of my job, part of me still wonders what it might have been like to have a less turbulent career. Deep down, I don't think it was ever in my constitution to work a 9 to 5 job. I wasn't built to fit in a box.

I'm still chasing sunsets, though the horizon appears to get closer every day. On that nearing horizon, I have fantasies of spending more time with my children and grandchildren, having more time with a guitar in my hand, traveling with a band, learning to play the piano, and seeing a few of my books and songs published. As I chase these sunsets, and watch the glowing orb sink below the horizon, I can't help but reflect on all that has transpired to reach this altitude. I think it's only at this height where you achieve perspective.

The best part of my life, which has taken me higher than any aircraft I have been blessed to pilot, has been watching my two children become successful independent members of a society that is increasingly difficult to navigate and understand.

At this altitude, you begin to see how even the most difficult parts of life were opportunities for learning and growth. I know the joy of a successful relationship, but I also understand the pain of how a relationship can switch, change, and spin out of control.

I've carried the hurt of being abandoned by my father at an early age; yet this sorrow was the catalyst that pushed me to build self-confidence and likely prodded me into a life of determination and persistence that has served me well. I've said throughout my career that you can learn as much from a bad captain as a good captain, and I hope what I have learned has helped me to captain my children with a much more positive experience.

I find myself overwhelmed with gratitude to finally understand my mother and the challenges she faced while single-handedly raising us. It took time, perhaps more than it should have, for me to recognize the disappointments I carried were not a reflection of her shortcomings. Instead, they were a testament of my own struggle to comprehend the immense sacrifices she made, striving to play the roles of both mother and father. Her success in this endeavor was nothing short of remarkable. I have few regrets in my life, but one of them is that when my mother passed away in July 2021, she may not have known how appreciative I was, and am, for her many sacrifices.

I regret that my siblings and I were raised in a manner where showing love was not normalized. I think we all love each other and would do anything we could to help one another, but we just weren't raised to do it outwardly and publicly. There is no animosity or resentment, just a lack of the close-knit family feeling. Being the oldest, I wish now that I would have done more to provide leadership to my siblings. My little sister Jeannette looked up to me as a father figure, but it was not until close to her death in November 2020, that I realized it. While we were all close in age, my younger sisters may have had to grow up quicker than I did. I wish I could have demonstrated to them the maturity they probably needed from me at that young and tender age. Perhaps it was this overwhelming responsibility that made me seek out the machine shed as a 14-year-old boy. Perhaps I wasn't only trying to escape western Nebraska, but a childhood that wasn't pictured on any Hallmark cards.

But I'm thankful for a childhood that wasn't picture perfect. I'm thankful for the 14-year-old boy who just wanted to escape into the sky. I escaped western Nebraska only to end up in eastern Nebraska, but in between, I was privileged to see the whole world. Where we take off is never as important as where we land.

As the nose of the aircraft in relation to the horizon is a constant in aviation, so is the ability to learn from—not live in—the past, and understand that tomorrow has all the possibilities with absolutely none of the promises. I want to keep moving forward, my eyes searching the horizon line for whatever possibility may come next.

Ladies and gentlemen, this is your captain speaking. We are now beginning our descent into the last sentences of this book. Please ensure your seatbelts are securely fastened, your seatbacks and tray tables are in the upright position, and all carry-on items are stowed underneath the seat in front of you or in the overhead bins.

I would like to thank you for choosing to spend time with me on your journey today. I hope you have found something in this book that you will take with you. Like the seat cushions that can be used as flotation devices, this book also has multiple uses: entertainment, door stop, coaster, or a very poor flotation device.

On behalf of the entire crew, thank you for flying with me. It has been my pleasure to travel with you on this part of your journey, and I hope you have a pleasant stay or safe travels to your final destination.

Acknowledgments

No book is written by an author alone. We are indebted to many people who helped us streamline a hunk of jumbled words into something ready to fly. Rick and Pam Collins, without your encouragement and support, this book would still be grounded. Thank you for believing that a bunch of half-baked stories could be shaped into a coherent memoir. Kerwin Donis, you read an early draft of this book and didn't allow us to settle with good enough. Thank you for pushing us to soar farther and higher. Brianna Rowe, our eagle-eyed editor, thank you for your abundant love of semicolons, which could only be matched by our abundant love of run-on sentences. Your expertise improved our writing by leaps and bounds. Poe Ballantine, we are honored you read our book and lifted us up with such kind words. Trevor Schmidt, we are blessed with your legal expertise, and Anna is blessed beyond measure to share her life with you. Tierney, Caris, and Logan Schmidt, thank you for only rolling your eyes a little when your mom read sections of this book out loud ad nauseum. Katie Spirko and Rob Osborn, you've turned into amazing adults despite the parenting you received from a wayward pilot who wasn't anything close to normal. Kenny Groves, though only a few months older than Donald, you have served as both a friend and father figure. Either by setting an incredibly poor example of what to do, or a very good example of what not to do, you helped Donald navigate through life in more ways than you'll ever know. A great debt of gratitude is owed to the countless pilots, instructors, flight attendants, mechanics, and gate agents who played a part in my aviation career. And to all those whose names appear within these pages, thank you; or I'm sorry, depending on where you land.